PERSPECTIVES ON WRITING
Series Editor, Susan H. McLeod

PERSPECTIVES ON WRITING
Series Editor, Susan H. McLeod

The Perspectives on Writing series addresses writing studies in a broad sense. Consistent with the wide ranging approaches characteristic of teaching and scholarship in writing across the curriculum, the series presents works that take divergent perspectives on working as a writer, teaching writing, administering writing programs, and studying writing in its various forms.

The WAC Clearinghouse and Parlor Press are collaborating so that these books will be widely available through free digital distribution and low-cost print editions. The publishers and the Series editor are teachers and researchers of writing, committed to the principle that knowledge should freely circulate. We see the opportunities that new technologies have for further democratizing knowledge. And we see that to share the power of writing is to share the means for all to articulate their needs, interest, and learning into the great experiment of literacy.

Recent Books in the Series

Katherine V. Wills and Rich Rice (Eds.), *ePortfolio Performance Support Systems: Constructing, Presenting, and Assessing Portfolios* (2013)

Mike Duncan and Star Medzerian Vanguri (Eds.), *The Centrality of Style* (2013)

Chris Thaiss, Gerd Bräuer, Paula Carlino , Lisa Ganobcsik-Williams, and Aparna Sinha (Eds.), *Writing Programs Worldwide: Profiles of Academic Writing in Many Places* (2012)

Andy Kirkpatrick and Zhichang Xu, *Chinese Rhetoric and Writing: An Introduction for Language Teachers* (2012)

Doreen Starke-Meyerring, Anthony Paré, Natasha Artemeva, Miriam Horne, and Larissa Yousoubova (Eds.), *Writing in Knowledge Societies* (2011)

Martine Courant Rife, Shaun Slattery, and Dànielle Nicole DeVoss (Eds.), *Copy(write): Intellectual Property in the Writing Classroom* (2011)

David Franke, Alex Reid, and Anthony Di Renzo (Eds.), *Design Discourse: Composing and Revising Programs in Professional and Technical Writing* (2010)

A RHETORIC OF LITERATE ACTION: LITERATE ACTION VOLUME 1

Charles Bazerman

The WAC Clearinghouse
wac.colostate.edu
Fort Collins, Colorado

Parlor Press
www.parlorpress.com
Anderson, South Carolina

The WAC Clearinghouse, Fort Collins, Colorado 80523-1052

Parlor Press, 3015 Brackenberry Drive, Anderson, South Carolina 29621

Printed in the United States of America

Library of Congress Cataloging-in-Publication Data

Bazerman, Charles.
   A Rhetoric of Literate Action : Literate Action volume 1 / Charles Bazerman.
      pages cm. -- (Perspectives on Writing)
   Includes bibliographical references and index.
   ISBN 978-1-60235-473-9 (pbk. : acid-free paper) -- ISBN 978-1-60235-474-6 (hardcover : acid-free paper) -- ISBN 978-1-60235-475-3 (adobe ebook) -- ISBN 978-1-60235-476-0 (epub)
   1. Rhetoric. 2. Written communication. I. Title.
   P301.B365 2013
   808--dc23
                              2013033946

Copyeditor: Don Donahue
Designer: Mike Palmquist
Series Editor: Susan H. McLeod

This book is printed on acid-free paper.

The WAC Clearinghouse supports teachers of writing across the disciplines. Hosted by Colorado State University, it brings together scholarly journals and book series as well as resources for teachers who use writing in their courses. This book is available in digital format for free download at http://wac.colostate.edu.

Parlor Press, LLC is an independent publisher of scholarly and trade titles in print and multimedia formats. This book is available in paperback, cloth, and Adobe eBook formats from Parlor Press at http://www.parlorpress.com. For submission information or to find out about Parlor Press publications, write to Parlor Press, 3015 Brackenberry Drive, Anderson, South Carolina 29621, or e-mail editor@parlorpress.com.

CONTENTS

A RHETORIC OF LITERATE ACTION: LITERATE ACTION VOLUME 1

INTRODUCTION

Writing can seem an amorphous task. Writers seem to fill blank pages with inventions of endless possibilities—from cookbooks and instructions for the latest electronic gadget to prayer books and legal codes, from corporate reports on emerging markets and botanic treatises on leaf veins of deciduous trees to undergraduate papers for history courses and personal diaries of self-doubts. How do people do this amazing variety of things through writing? What can we say that would help us do these things more effectively?

Indeed the variety seems so great that general advice or analysis seems quixotic, and we ought to focus only on specific kinds of writing. One might be able to say something useful about historically-evolved cookbooks, and how one might go about producing one that speaks to the commercial market in the United States in the early twenty-first century. We have learned things about technical writing, business, and legal writing that have helped inform writing education of professionals in each of these domains. Research and pedagogy in Writing Across the Curriculum, in the Disciplines and Professions, and in the Workplace have guided approaches for developing writing of many specific types.

If the writing task is specific enough, detailed instructions can direct the text's completion, such as filling out a government form properly (at least in the particular version of the form used in a particular year)—very detailed specifications tell us what we should write in each box and our writing choices are limited as to which address or ethnicity we might report. Even if the form contains a more open-ended narrative, such as in a grant application, often the material that needs to be covered and the order it should be covered in are directed by instructions and regulations. Such narrowed focus helps direct our work, but it also limits our thinking, expression, identities, and commitments. In the extreme cases of filling out forms we can become powerless subjects of bureaucratic definitions and regulations.

Yet writing can be a powerful tool of thinking, feeling, identity, commitment, and action. In turning our impulses into words, we can reveal ourselves to ourselves and to the world, and we can take place in important debates, movements, and activities. Writing forms the playing fields of our literate times and each piece of writing we do claims a place, identity, meaning, and action on those fields of life. The more we can write beyond the bounds of constrained bureaucratic prescriptions, the more we gain power to define and represent ourselves in the literate world.

But the problem of writing seems so amorphous that once we step out of highly directed, highly instructed writing situations we may quickly feel at sea, not knowing which direction to take and without signs to help us gain our bearings and make decisions. Even if we are released on a small confined, pond, such as writing a paper for a university political science course on political parties where we are told what ideas to refer to and which cases to discuss, we may still struggle to know which direction to go in.

Of course, in writing an essay for a political science course, the more we know about political science, the longer we have been in the course and have known the professor, the more political science papers we have read and written, the more we have learned the vocabulary and read the literature of political science and the historical accounts of political parties, and the more we know the genres of the field, then the more effectively and efficiently we can address the task. Yet underlying questions remain about what we want to accomplish and how we can do it in more deeply effective ways; that is, we cannot reduce our writing just to type, but must create it anew from our interests, resources, thoughts, and perceptions.

What would be useful in this and many other circumstances is a way of understanding our writing situation and what we might do with it—not just how writing is generally done in these circumstances but how we might transform the circumstances through our participation. This volume, *A Rhetoric of Literate Action*, offers an approach to understanding writing situations and how we can respond creatively in deep and transformative ways, because we understand the game and our moves more deeply. The first four chapters of this volume provide a framework for identifying and understanding the situations writing comes out of and is directed toward. The next four chapters then consider how a text works to transform a situation and achieve the writer's motives as the text begins to take form. The final four chapters provide more specific advice of the work to be accomplished in bringing the text to final form and how to manage the work and one's own emotions and energies so as to accomplish the work most effectively.

The advice of this book is for the experienced writer with a substantial repertoire of skills, and now would find it useful to think in more fundamental strategic terms about what they want their texts to accomplish, what form the texts might take, how to develop specific contents, and how to arrange the work of writing. While the book contains some comments identifying challenges of developing writers and writers at social margins with an eye to how a writer can strategically address these challenges, those topics will not be at the center of discussion so as to maintain focus on strategic choice-making experienced writers,

Likewise, I will from time to time discuss collaborative writing processes, problems of multiple audiences, and the effects of changing technologies on writing, how to accomplish it, and what its impact is. To keep an already complicated and multidimensional subject as simple as I can, however, I will predominantly attend to the actions of individual experienced writers expressing their views and interests to readers, who each read one at a time, though from their social and organizational locations and interests. As should be evident from the presentation in this and the companion volume, the view of writing presented here is deeply dialogic, interactive, and social, but still writing and reading are done predominantly in semi-privacy, as readers and writers engage in their own thoughts in relation to the text, often for extended periods. Even in highly interactive collaborative processes, each participant must look inward to understand and evaluate the meanings evoked by the inscribed words. Further, writers aim to evoke meanings in individual readers, even though readers may be parts of teams or organizations, and readers attribute those evoked meanings as the expression of a writer, even if that writer is buried within complex corporate processes. In any event, what is here said about individuals can be, with care, extrapolated to more complex group processes.

Finally, while I will make some mention of multimedia and other communicative changes that are part of the digital age, the focus will be on the written word. The written word still maintains importance in digital environments, and we live in a world given shape by literacy. While the digital revolution is transforming our communicative and social environment, it is hard to know exactly what these changes will look like in even a few decades. What does seem clear though, is that the written word will maintain an important role for the foreseeable future and that the social changes will grow on a foundation established by the literate transformation of the past centuries. So it is of value for us to get our bearings in the written world as we venture forward into new communicative environments.

In providing advice about how to understand one's communicative situation and respond strategically to it, this volume follows in the long tradition of books of rhetoric, from the time of Aristotle until today, but with some substantial differences, as I will discuss at the end of the first chapter. So as not to encumber the practical orientation of the book, I will keep references to a minimum and cite sources only when they will directly contribute to exposition of the advice. A fully-documented companion volume, *A Theory of Literate Action*, examines the sources and theoretical reasoning behind the rhetoric and places its understanding of language, utterance, and writing within a wider social scientific understanding of humans, society, knowledge, communications, and literacy. While there is not a one-to-one match between the topics and chapters of the two books, the introduction of the companion volume identifies chapters where some of the ideas from the first volume are elaborated in the second.

I would like to thank the many people who over the years have responded to the emerging ideas expressed here. In particular I would like to thank Anis Bawarshi, Joshua Compton, Christiane Donahue, David Russell, Sandra Thompson, and the anonymous reviewers of the WAC Clearinghouse for their thoughtful readings and comments on draft chapters of both volumes. Finally I owe endless gratitude to my partner of over forty years, Shirley Geoklin Lim.

CHAPTER 1

RHETORICS OF SPEAKING AND WRITING

Speech was born in human interaction. It coordinates activities ("Lift . . . now"), perceptions ("Look at that bird"), and knowledge of things not immediately perceivable ("many fish are in the river in the next valley"). It also leads people to modify their own behavior and/or states of mind on the basis of the procedures, perceptual categories, and knowledge first received or developed in social interaction. Further, speech articulates the categories by which people may be held socially accountable and provides the means by which people may give accounts of their actions ("If I do this, what would I tell people?") Such realized potentials of language have proved of immense evolutionary advantage and have become key elements in our sociality and culture. By providing the means to create shared accounts of where we have been and where we are headed, it has made history and future culturally present. The beliefs, accounts, plans, and modes of social organization of oral cultures are cast into a different mode when writing enters.

Although speech and language go back to the beginning of human life, writing is generally thought to have been invented around 5000 years ago (Schmandt-Bessarat, 1992), simultaneous with the development of urban economies, larger political organizations, extensive religions, and many social institutions that have come to characterize the modern world (Goody, 1986).

Human language is built on interaction and activity in context and becomes meaningful and purposeful only in use. Internalized language as well originates in interpersonal interactions and has consequences for our internal self-regulation, using the culturally available categories and imperatives of language (Vygotsky, 1986). Our internal thoughts then reemerge, reformulated in processes of externalization to make ourselves intelligible to others (Mead 1934; Volosinov, 1973; Vygotsky, 1986). People regularly experience externalization as helping them know what they are thinking and clarifying what it is they think. Our later inventions that facilitate communication at a distance grow out of the same socio-cognitive resources and motivations as spoken language—whether fire signals or writing; whether cheap paper or computer screens; whether telegraphy, telephony, or the Internet; whether mail distribution systems or chat rooms; whether a tyrant's stone tablets in the center of town or a commercial publishing industry. As the means and reach of communication change, our thinking, feeling, and motives may transform and grow in response to the new opportunities; our minds and societies are plastic and creative. But the creativity almost always is intertwined with our fundamental communicative capacities and orientations.

Thus to come to terms with writing and how to do it, we need to understand it both within the human capacity for language and in the social-cultural-historical conditions which have developed dialectically with our writing practices. Considering how we successfully manage to use language in face-to-face interaction will help us understand the challenges we must overcome in order to communicate when we are no longer in the same time and location to coordinate our meanings and actions with each other. In short, a fundamental problem in writing is to be able to understand and recreate the social circumstance and social interaction which the communication is part of, but which is obscured by the transmission of the words over time and space from one apparent set of social circumstances to another. We can understand much about writing if we understand how writing overcomes this difficulty, to help us locate our written communications in socio-cultural history, where written messages are coming from, and where they are going to.

FACE-TO-FACE SPEECH

Face-to-Face speech, the condition within which language developed historically, occurs in a specific shared time and place. We speak to the people in front of us, as part of the events unfolding before us, in response to the comments we have just heard. We speak in the clothes we have worn that day and in the roles, statuses, and relationships we inhabit among those people we speak with. We see and feel all this in our bodies, viscerally. Seeing where we are, we react and speak. We say hello to a neighbor, good morning to a lover, and "I'll take care of that right now Ms. Johnson, immediately" to our boss.

In these moments of immediate transactions we can make distant people and events imaginatively present by mentioning them. "Remember Mr. Jawari? You know, Jackie's teacher. Well, I saw him over at the mall yesterday . . ." Or we can have distant unmentioned circumstances and relations in our minds, influencing how we talk and what we talk about. We may remember our parents telling us how to behave in public as we meet new neighbors. Our response to a sales pitch can be tempered by thinking about our vanishing bank account. Similarly our interlocutors name things they want to remind us of or show us for the first time. We may sometimes even guess (though not necessarily accurately) the urgencies and exigencies in their own life that stand behind their behavior and talk ("Why are they mentioning this to me now?"). But these non-present presences need to be evoked and mutually acknowledged in the conversation for them to be part of the meanings and activities realized in the here and now of talk (Sacks, 1995). That is, only when the child's teacher or the empty bank account are mentioned and oriented to by the people talking together do they become a shared object of attention, a topic of conversation—otherwise they remain private individual orientations open only to speculation by our interlocutors about what was on our mind.

A central problem and task of spoken interaction is alignment within a shared communicative space. Alignment starts with the initiating task of gaining the attention of the one we wish to talk to and continues as people attend toward each other and what they may be conveying. People look at each other or stare toward the same point in space. Their bodies take mutually responsive postures—opening toward each other or backing away, arms folding in similar positions or gesturing into the space between. They also align to each other's speech patterns—coordinating turns, adopting similar and coordinated rhythms and intonations, adjusting to each other's accents and dialects (Chafe, 1994). Further, they align to each other's meanings projected into the public space of talk. They take up common referents, themes, and knowledge introduced into the talk by prior speakers, they adopt mutually confirming assumptions (Sachs, 1995). They take what has been said as a given—both as meaning and action. Indeed, in the way they take up and use what has been said before they retrospectively interpret and create the continuing meaning of previous utterances.

Alignment is so crucial to the maintenance of conversation that people regularly and consistently repair the talk when they feel that there has been some breach that will disrupt the flow of talk, the social alignment of participants, or the mutual coordination of meanings (Schegloff et al., 1977). Unless the talk is repaired, the conversation can break and participants fall away. Such repairs may correct misunderstandings, such as who was being discussed, but can also involve backing away from something that was previously placed in the shared space of interaction. Saying something was only meant as a joke or is not really important indicates that what had been mentioned previously ought not to be attended to as the interaction moves forward.

Through alignment of speech activities, referents, interactional roles and relations, speech participants create a mutually recognized space of interaction, which has been called footing (Goffman, 1981) or frame (Goffman, 1974; Tannen, 1993). This footing goes beyond the recognition of the physical space and set of participants one is within to giving it a particular social characterization or shape. Thus by the change of posture or a few words one can reorient the attention of a group engaged in a political argument to a shared moment of satirical laughter, and then into a discussion of comics. Or if one person indicates by facial gesture that he hears another's comments as an insult, all eyes focus on the social conflict and leave the substance of the discussion behind. This reorientation from one kind of scene to another is facilitated because we come to recognize patterned kinds of social scenes, interactions, and utterances. We see events as similar to other events and recognize them as of a kind, or genre.

The social understandings evoked in the speech-mediated framings can even change perception and definition of the visible material event (Hanks, 1996). As one person starts to recount a recent injury, a previously unnoticed discoloring of the skin begins to loom large and become visible as a bruise. An intimate interactive space can suddenly be opened up when one of the participants waves to a friend across the street.

CODES AND CONTEXTS

In daily life, we come to use and understand language within specific events, shaped by the language as the events unfold. We use language on the fly as part of emerging interactional dramas that change with every new word uttered. Yet when we study or think about language, we look at it in a very different way, focusing on the small components we carry across many kinds of situations—the recognizably different sounds, the words, the organization of words into propositions. Linguistic prescriptions and descriptions share this atomized view of language, which then is reproduced in grammars and dictionaries—the practical tools that popularly represent knowledge of a language, but stripped of use in particular interactions.

Early learning of a first spoken language, as developmental linguists point out, however, occurs largely in face-to-face interaction among already competent language users of the community. Children may show at certain moments of development an awareness of the code as code—asking repeatedly "what is that?" as they begin to amass words, or as they hyper-correct and then soften grammatical regularities as a result of increasing information. However, spoken first language use and learning is much less a reflective and codified experience as it is an accumulation of situated practical experiences in the course of daily interaction.

The study of written language has been dominated by code concerns—writing systems, spelling, grammar, generalized word meanings, organizational patterns. This abstracted view of written language may have partly emerged because written texts come from beyond the immediate social situation, specifically to allow travel to different times and places. Thus writing appears have a kind of contextlessness, which might be better characterized as trans-contextedness. Communication at a distance through writing certainly has burdens of being interpretable without all the supporting apparatus of face-to-face interaction; it also has a further burden of creating an interactional context at a distance that makes the communication meaningful and consequential.

The linguistic, educational, interpretive, and regulatory practices that have developed around writing have reinforced the impression of a contextless code with universal meaning carried within the text, as long as that code was competently understood and produced. Formal language instruction developed first in the transmission of dead classical languages—that is, language which is not learned in ordinary meaningful communications in interaction with live speakers. Further these classical languages were used to access texts distant from the immediate culture for a kind of transcultural, universalized veneration, or for the maintenance of universal truths embodied in sacred texts. The coincident development of printing, state bureaucracies, and cultural hegemonies in the East and West fostered additionally code regulation—regulation of characters and spelling, morphology, and syntax. This code-regulation was enforced and rewarded through systems of class and power to create cultures of correctness that again appeared as contextless markers of legitimacy to be on display in every situation.

COMMUNICATION AT A DISTANCE

Yet written language can gain its meanings only as part of meaningful social interactions. An uncontexted snippet of written code is no more meaningful than an unidentified snippet of audiotape—probably less because we have fewer clues of where it came from (through accent or background sounds) and interaction (through multiple speakers, intonation, rhythm, and the like). We can gain a glimpse of this problem if we consider the difficulties people have in interpreting archeological fragments of texts. The interpretation rests not just on breaking the code, but on reconstructing the context of use within which the utterance was meaningful—often a very local context of a farmer's granary or a merchant's counting house.

As writing began to carry messages across distances and situations, it was delivered with visible symbols of its social meaning. Early messengers would carry the signs of authority of the message senders, would speak in the name of the king or other sender, and would command the respect granted to the sender. Thus not only the message, but the social arrangements were extended over distance.

Even such spare communications at a distance as the signal fires that carried the news of the end of the Trojan War, as recounted in the *Iliad*, depended on enormous social contexting to be meaningful. The signaling enterprise only made sense in the context of the end of a momentous war, the return of troops from a distance, and the interests of the Greeks at home. It was only made possible by organizing a widespread group of individuals, carefully placed at sites visible to other selected sites, and aligned to the task of noting and reproducing fire. Finally, its interpretation depended on the initiators and receivers having a shared, prearranged meaning of the symbol. Two millennia later, when the French created a nationwide system of semaphore telegraphs, they needed an entire bureaucracy to manage the signal, direct the messages to appropriate parties, and create contexts of meaning for the messages, which served a limited range of defined military purposes. Smoke signals and talking drums equally are embedded within well-focused and aligned systems of relations, communications, meanings, and social moments.

In the later half of the nineteenth century the telephone opened opportunities for vocal communication at a distance, soon fostering focused, recognizable contexts of uses and means of signaling those contexts. At first U.S. telephone companies were small and local with a limited number of subscribers already familiar with each other, for example within a town. The telephone communications simply carried on and extended pre-existing relationships, largely business—and thus each telephonic transaction was well-embedded within a familiar set of business arrangements. Even then, telephone companies needed to offer instruction in a new etiquette for initiating conversations, identifying parties speaking, and introducing the specific occasion and transaction (Fischer, 1992). As the telephone uses expanded to social calling, further etiquettes were needed to signify the call.

Today any experienced user of the telephone can rapidly recognize the source and nature of the many calls we now receive from even unknown callers, including fund raising, sales, and political calls. Recognizable contexts have emerged in the patterns of individual calls, typical transactions, on-going networks of relations, and organizational structures that have developed around the phone, including banks of commercial callers, phone hotlines, emergency services, polling organizations, phone-order sales, and product help. The importance of establishing those contexts of meaning is made salient to us every time we make a mistake and misattribute a call for a few moments, until we realize that this is not a friendly call from a neighbor, but a fund raising call for the youth organization; that this is not an independent call from an independent polling agency, but a political pitch from an interest group.

Similarly, sound recording developed an entertainment industry, on one side, with highly genred products offering anticipatable messages, activities, and amusements to be invoked on appropriate occasions, with a rapidly developing etiquette—where and when it was acceptable or desirable to play which kind of recording at what volume. On the business side, recording technologies developed for individualized, contexted messages, such as a reminder to oneself or dictation for one's secretary. These highly localized messages have specific meanings for identifiable people in specific relation to the person recording the message, often within a specific time frame. Now digital technologies have facilitated a proliferation of personally produced sound and video files which are developing their new kinds, functions, circulation, and etiquettes—and thus anticipatibility and means of interpretation.

Presidential speeches to the public via radio and television are a good example of how contexts are provided, even beyond the well-understood relation of a leader speaking to constituencies. Annual "State of the Nation" reports to the legislature provided one kind of forum, and speeches on national crises, another. The broadcast press conference grew out of journalistic interview practices, and bear much of the flavor of reporters going after stories and an office holder defending policies and practices in the face of inquiry. But when during the Depression the U.S. President Franklin Roosevelt wanted to use the radio to create a more direct and regular channel to the citizens, he recreated a fireside atmosphere evoking intimacy of the head of households gathering families together. Such regular messages of hope and planning, addressing problems in a calm everyday manner, have developed a new kind of context of mass intimacy of leadership. Only insofar as that bond of trusting intimacy is maintained are such messages meaningful.

Writing, of course, was among the earliest forms of communication at a distance and has become the most extensive, diverse, and pliable of means of communication at a distance—even as the medium of delivery has changed from a messenger bearing a letter to mass-marketed publications, to digital packets flowing over the internet. To develop a rhetoric of writing, to understand what we must accomplish to write successfully, we need to address how writing communicates at a distance, how it can create contexts of meaningful interaction, and how it can speak to the contexts it evokes and participates in. There are some uses of writing that have no greater distance than face-to-face conversation, as when people sitting next to each other pass notes in response to a lecturer's comments—an ironic "sure" scribbled. But even if the note is to be passed across the room, it would need to display much of the context that would have vanished by the time the note reached its destination. The note would at least have to indicate who wrote it and who was to receive it as well what the offending words were to remind the reader on the other side of the room of what was said five minutes ago that so exercised his ironic friend.

RHETORIC AND WRITING

The problem of context is crucial to writing, yet it is elusive. Writing comes to us on pieces of paper or digital screens that look very much one like another, obscuring where the message may have come from, where it was intended to go, and what purpose it was intended to carry out in what circumstances. If texts travel through time and space, where is their context? Do they make their own contexts, which they then speak to? Unless we have means to address such questions, our approaches to understanding what to write and the meaning of others' writings are limited to issues of code (spelling, vocabulary, grammar, syntax, and style) and decontextualized meanings (imagining such things could in fact exist). The answers to these questions will give us the basis on which to form a rhetoric for written language, a rhetoric which will differ in significant ways from the traditional one formed around problems of high-stakes public speech in political and deliberative contexts.

Rhetoric is the reflective practical art of strategic utterance in context from the point of view of the participants, both speaker and hearer, writer and reader. That is, rhetoric helps us think about what we might most effectively use words to meet our ends in social interchange, and helps us think about what others through their words are attempting to do with us. The reflection is both productive, in leading to new utterance and further action, and critical in helping us evaluate what has already transpired, presumably with an eye toward future practice—knowing what stances to take to others and widening our repertoire and reflective capabilities to act knowingly. While rhetoric as a field of study has also developed analytical and philosophic components and many rhetorical scholars see themselves primarily as theorists, the field is founded on human communicative practice and its value to society is in its ability to support more effective, more thoughtful practice. The theories presented in this and the companion volume are, therefore, committed to this end rather than the resolution of theoretical problems, though many theoretical problems may need to be addressed along the way.

Rhetoric differs in substantial ways from the other disciplines of language, first because it does not take disembodied code as its starting point. Code, for rhetoric, is a resource to be deployed in concrete situations for individual and communal purposes and activities, which are the primary concern. Similarly, abstracted meanings that might be deployed in any situation are secondary to the purpose and effect they are used for. Meanings do not exist as fixed absolutes within themselves and the signs used to evoke them, but to be deployed, constructed, imaginatively evoked, as the rhetor's purposes and strategic plan in particular situations warrant. Meanings and truths arise in the course of human inquiry and activity.

Rhetoric is also different from the other arts of language because it adopts the point of view of the users, rather than the unengaged stance of the analyst of the code. Rhetoric is built for action, rather than static description. Rhetoric's fundamental questions have to do with how to accomplish things, rather than what things are. How language works in context is worth knowing because it lets you know how to use it. The concepts are ones that help you locate yourself in the activity, define your concerns, and recognize and mobilize resources for interaction.

Thus rhetoric is strategic and situational, based on the purposes, needs, and possibilities of the user, the resources available then and there to be deployed, and the potentialities of the situation. While rhetoric identifies some general processes and resources of communicative interaction, these are tools to understand local situations and heuristics in helping the speaker decide what to say, how to say it, and how to go about constructing the statement. Rhetoric is cast in terms of purposes and possibilities and future outcomes. It supports activity informed by goals rather than at already finished objects. Even the completed text to be critically analyzed is considered in its social, persuasive effects and not its pure textuality. Further the critical analysis has its own further purposes, such as to delegitimate the words of an opponent or to understand effective strategies to be used in future situations. Yet none of these trajectories of action is certain in their outcomes, for the outcomes depend on the purposes, actions, and trajectories of the audience and those who make further utterances.

Because rhetoric is concerned with trajectories of on-going situations from the point of view of the participants, it is also reflective, looking back onto oneself and one's co-participants. It helps us look at what is going on, so we can do it better. However, the mirror never takes us very far from the situation and our engagement in it. It only offers a bit of perspective with which to watch ourselves as we remain engaged. Rhetoric is an applied art, applied to ourselves, to direct our own courses of action. Even if professional rhetoricians give advice or instruction to clients, that advice only becomes of use as people themselves incorporate the advice or principles into their actions. There are limits to what a rhetorician can usefully advise in a general way beyond some conceptual categories for considering the situation without enquiring deeply of the person being advised about their situation, goals, resources and capabilities. When such an inquiry takes place, the rhetorician inevitably becomes a collaborator in the rhetor's thinking about and response to the situation.

Thus, what a rhetoric can most usefully offer, rather than specific prescriptions about what to say or write and how to say, is conceptual tools to ponder one's rhetorical situation and choices. If, however, situations are heavily constrained and practices typified and even regulated, then specific advice might be usefully given, but at the cost of constraining the writer's range of action and choices. In the extreme such advice takes the form of instruction manuals on how to fill out bureaucratic forms or directions to sales clerks on how to fill out the sales screens at the cashier terminal. In such cases rhetorical choices are few and the writer's agency is limited. Professional style manuals that give guidance on how to produce work that meets the minimum standards of that profession also constrain by intention. Yet such style manuals leave substantial opportunities for the writer to express professional judgment and to influence what is said, and what meanings are conveyed within the regulated constraints—for otherwise it wouldn't be a profession.

The rhetoric offered in this volume, however, will not take for granted or foster any particular set of constraints or practices. Accordingly, it will not offer prescriptions or ready-made solutions for particular writing situations. Here, rather, I will attempt to create a rhetoric of wide generality, relevant to all written texts in all their historical and contemporary variety. This rhetoric will provide principles to understand any particular set of constraints and typified practices in any focused domain, and could be used to uncover the rhetorical logic in any set of instructions or style book. This rhetoric can help us see that those who construct the bureaucratic forms or compose the professional style manuals themselves exert extraordinary rhetorical power in shaping the situations, interactions, discourse, and meanings of others. This rhetoric will help us see how different social systems use writing to pursue their activities, and how we can act most effectively within them—potentially even bypassing, subverting, or transforming them through strategic action. While examples may be drawn from many domains, the constraints of any of them will not be taken as absolute or general, but only applicable in the specific situation. This rhetoric is aimed at recognizing the diversity of activities using writing that have developed over the five thousand years of literacy, and how we can effectively navigate in the complex literate world we now live into pursue our interests through the opportunities and resources at hand.

ORIGINS OF RHETORIC

Most societies have proverbial wisdom on how people should talk—implying a widespread recognition that one can reflect on one's language use to guide practice. One of my favorites is the central Asian adage, "If you are going to tell the truth, you should have one foot in the stirrup." But the most extensive and prominent reflection on strategic communication arose in ancient Greece and Rome. The vigorous tradition of classical rhetoric developed fundamental concepts of rhetorical situations and how situations can be addressed. As well it identified some of the fundamental resources available to speakers and the ways in which language works upon people. A number of the concepts and resources of classical rhetoric will be important within this and the companion volume. However, classical rhetoric was concerned with only a limited range of culturally embedded practices, all of which were oral and political, involving high-stakes contentions. Its primary concerns were the public speeches of the agora or market place addressing criminal guilt and innocence (forensic rhetoric), matters of public policy (deliberative rhetoric), or celebration of the state, communal values, and rhetorical artfulness (epideictic rhetoric). The rhetorical analysis of situations, the kinds of goals, the anticipated interactive processes, the resources considered available, and the media of communication all were shaped around the agora. These forms of rhetoric are most directly applicable to speechmaking in successor institutions, often consciously modeled on classical forms: courts, legislatures, and political gatherings. Nonetheless, these institutions have changed radically by literate practices as courts of law have now become saturated with written precedents, filings, briefs, records, and other texts and legislatures must deal with lengthy bills, technical reports of commissions, paperwork generated by office staff and government bureaucracies, and journalistic accounts that reach a wider public sphere.

Furthermore, many domains of speech in the ancient world were not brought under rhetorical scrutiny, were not made the object of a discipline of strategic reflection. Sales talk in the marketplace, although likely filled with a wide folk repertoire of tricks and stances, remained outside the purview of classic rhetoric. The language of commerce had to await the rise of business schools and the marketing professions (themselves tied to the rise of wide-circulation periodicals and large industrial corporations with extended markets) to become systematically considered. Similarly, talk with intimates (though we presume it went on in the classical world) was not the object of professional attention until the twentieth century, except for risqué poetic advice in the *ars amoris* tradition.

Moreover, although literacy was widespread in Greece and Rome by the time systematic rhetoric arose and despite the fact that rhetorical manuals were written, very little attention was given to how one should write, except as a means of scripting oral production (as Plato derides in the Phaedrus). Some passing remarks were made on the style appropriate for letters, and a separate smaller tradition of *ars poetica* arose, but the problems of how to write largely remained unexamined.

Since then periodic attempts to consider writing rhetorically and to extend the genres and concerns of rhetoric beyond high-stakes public argumentation have been limited and have not yet resulted in a fully rhetorical consideration of written communication. In the Middle Ages, the *ars dicitaminas* and *ars notaria* were systematic attempts to consider letter and document writing. Despite enduring consequences for bureaucracy, law, business contracts, and accountancy, they have had little long-term impact on canonical rhetorical teaching. In the Renaissance rhetoric attended to stylistic refinement that suggests a kind of word-crafting and revision facilitated by writing, but there was no attention to the fundamental problems of communication posed by writing.

In the eighteenth century, the emergence of natural philosophy, public journals, and new social ideologies—all of which decreased power of centralized elites and used writing to connect widespread but increasingly important publics—gave rise to attempts to reformulate rhetoric around the effect of texts on the sympathetic imaginations and understandings of readers, by such figures as Joseph Priestley, Adam Smith, and George Campbell. For a variety of ideological and institutional reasons, over the long term this broad reconsideration of rhetoric narrowed its focus to belles-lettristic rhetoric and became a precursor to literary studies, increasingly distanced from the discursive needs of daily situations and exercising power within the literate practices of modernity.

As the teaching of writing became a regular and widespread component of higher education in the late nineteenth century United States, another theory of written texts came to dominate education. This theory assumed a correlation between faculties of human understanding and a small number of patterns of textual exposition (known as the modes; Connors, 1981). The theory and the accompanying pedagogy did not attempt to contend with the wide range of social uses of writing, the many different social systems writing was part of, range of goals and interests of writers, or the variety of potential readers with different interests and different situations. That is, as a rhetoric, while reflective of individual understanding (according to a particular psychological theory), it was not strategic or situational. It rather assumed a constrained uniformity of understanding, activities, and goals. This limited range of rhetorical activities were congruent with the discourse practiced in the expanding university in the United States during the period between the Civil War and World War II, aimed at producing a professional class of managers, based on a model that ideologically foregrounded individuality and dispassionate reason and suppressed contention and difference of interest. As the teaching of writing moved away from the rhetorical tradition, in the U.S. in the early twentieth century, speech communication, which remained grounded in classical rhetoric, split from English Departments (Parker, 1967).

Even though classical rhetoric with some modern additions has been reintroduced into the teaching of writing in the U.S (for examples, Corbett, 1965; Crowley & Hawhee, 1994), it would benefit from a fresh reconceptualization around the problems of written communication, with an awareness of the social complexity of contemporary literate society, and deeply incorporating recent social theory and social science. Attempts at reconceptualizing rhetoric on more recent intellectual grounds have in fact been rife since the middle of the twentieth century. Fogarty (1959) in his philosophically oriented *Roots for A New Rhetoric* draws on mid-century conceptualizations of language and representation from Richards, Burke, and Korzybski. Fogarty, however, does not succeed in synthesizing these into a fresh rhetoric with clear practical consequences for writing. Perelman and Olbrechts-Tyteca (1969) in their *New Rhetoric* reinterpret Aristotle through legal reasoning and practice. Christensen (1969) grounds his *Notes Towards a New Rhetoric* in linguistics and stylistics to make new proposals on sentence style. Of these and the many others using the term "new rhetoric" the only one who bases his reconceptualization particularly on the problems of writing is Beale (1989) in *A Pragmatic Theory of Rhetoric*, though he still identifies his theory as fundamentally Aristotelian and he proceeds on predominantly Aristotelian theoretical and philosophic grounds. This volume directed at rhetorical writing practice and its companion elaborating the intellectual sources of the proposed theory attempt a more radical rethinking of rhetoric based on the problematics of writing and grounded in the thinking of contemporary social sciences, as elaborated in the companion volume.

With increasing rapidity over recent centuries and decades, new social forces have transformed social and cultural assumptions, distribution of work and communications, political and economic arrangements. Social and economic activities have become ever more thoroughly pervaded by literacy and symbolic manipulation—so that people now characterize us as within an information age, information that is multiple and global in origin. At the university discourse has become more complex and reflective, with prior social and cultural assumptions embedded in standard discursive practices increasingly questioned. More narrowly, in the last half century within a reinvigorated discipline of teaching of writing, research and theory has been drawing on wider ranges of social sciences, cultural studies, and humanities and has been addressing a wider range of writing practices in the university, the polity, the economy, and society. While many new lines of thinking about writing have developed, these have yet to be fully articulated in a coherent overview of strategic writing. The most successful model of writing set against the previous pedagogic traditions of modes and forms has been of the writing process, which is a theory of managing how one goes about writing, as an individual and as part of groups. This work, grounded in classical rhetorical theory of invention but adding to that experimental methods of cognitive science, has taken new directions because of the way in which writing supports drafting, revision, and editing—allowing one to hold on to and rework one's text, as well as to gain others readings perspectives and collaboration. However, process only covers part of what we must think about in writing—even in the oral classical rhetorical tradition, invention was only one of the five canons. The picture of writing drawn in this volume attempts to cover more of what we are starting to understand about writing. This will be a conceptual picture, to inform practical reflection on strategic communication, and thus insists on being considered as a rhetoric, even though it may not look much like previous books with that title. Because this volume considers writing as it manifests in the complexity of the modern world, it will employ many terms and concepts alien to the classical rhetorical tradition. It will deploy what we have been able to learn about the formation and dynamics of situations, the use of texts as active within situations, and the processes by which people interact, communicate, understand, formulate intentions, imagine, and create. And finally it will consider how we shape messages and create meanings within the genred spaces of the texts we write.

The next several chapters will consider where, when, and in which field of action we are writing for. Chapters 4 through 7 will consider the actions, motives, and strategies that give direction to our writing. Chapters 8 through 11 discuss the form our texts take, the meanings we invoke through the text, the experiences we create in our texts, and how we can bring the text to its fullest realization. The final chapter steps back from the text to consider the psychological processes and emotional complexities of writing, so we can understand and manage how we can produce texts with greatest success, least stress, and greatest satisfaction.

CHAPTER 2

KNOWING WHERE YOU ARE: GENRE

THE TEXTUAL MARKING OF SITUATIONALITY AND ACTIVITY

The fundamental problem in developing a rhetoric of writing is characterizing the situationality of written texts because writing so easily travels through space and time. Writing's asset of transportability means the written text can leave behind the physical location and moment in time when it was produced. It also escapes the immediate social circumstances, relations, and activities to affect different locales and activities at a distance, but these new locations are not visible in the immediate physical environs in which the text is produced. These new situations and interactions have to be constructed imaginatively by the writer and signaled adequately enough in the text for the reader to reconstruct them.

Letters provide a strong case in point, for they overtly announce their spatiality, temporality, relation, and activity. They typically announce the writer and intended receiver, and they are frequently dated and marked with the place of origin. They are generally intended for immediate use upon receipt and then either discarded or filed away as a memory aid or record of the now past transaction. Furthermore in salutation and signature they often specify the particular relation between the corresponding parties (terms of honor in the greeting and commitments of loyalty in the signature, for example). These relationships may be further specified ("I write you in your capacity as executor of the estate of . . ."; "I appeal to you as a fellow parent . . .") and bonds reinforced ("I hope all is well with you") in the course of the letter. Even more the substance of the letter may narrate the occasion that prompts the letter, the situation the letter speaks to, and the particular action the letter aims to complete ("I write in application for the position advertised in . . ."; "it has been many months since we have seen each other, and my thoughts repeatedly turn to your welfare, especially now that we hear reports of devastation in your land"; "Mom, my bank account is tapped out, please send money.")

Because the letter contains so many markers of its sociality, allowing the reader mentally to locate him or herself in the social interaction, it early on became one of the primary genres of writing. Starting with the explicit sociality of letters, many other written genres were able to find shape and meaning, until they became recognizable and recognized as distinctive forms—such as business reports, scientific journals, newspapers and magazines, and even financial instruments such as letters of credit, checks, and paper currency. It is not surprising, therefore, that the first rhetoric of writing concerned the writing of letters, the medieval *ars dictaminis* (Murphy, 1985). As a genre, or an increasingly distinctive set of genres, the letter asserts its place in the social world and helps formulate the sociality for many written documents (Bazerman, 1999b.)

Other early genres of writing relied on familiarity with well-known face-to-face oral performances, the memories of which were evoked by the written text. Special occasions, such as famous speeches, and everyday social events, such as the telling of tales, found their way onto the page, to be recreated by the reader. New texts could then be written drawing on the social understanding that accompanied such texts, both to prepare or script oral performance and to become new sorts of socio-literacy events, to be enacted during reading. Reading of play scripts, for example, is greatly enhanced if the reader has actually seen that play produced or even more, has rehearsed and performed the play—practices often invoked by teachers of dramatic literature. However, some texts such as some lyric poems or most philosophic treatises are written only to be read by the individual in isolation. Reading these texts requires entering into contemplative states of consciousness, oriented toward mental places abstracted from immediate physical circumstances to a world of ideas that seems to exist out of time.

Other uses for writing developed as part of well-structured activities, such as economic, legal, or governmental transactions. These provided strong contexts for the interpretation of texts and gave rise to regularized repetitive situations calling for similar utterances, producing familiar, recognizable genres that evoked relevant aspects of the entire activity system. For example, when you receive a monthly bill from the electric utility which is government regulated and taxed and you mail back a check with the bill stub, you rely on extensive institutional understanding of the government, the utility, the banking system, and your roles as a consumer, a householder, a citizen, and a financial agent. While much of this knowledge of these complex institutions remains in the background most of the time (especially now that this process is becoming automated through electronic billing directly to bank accounts), it is there to be invoked when relevant, such as when the utility sends you an unusually high bill or claims you have not been paying and threatens to cut off service.

These institutions with their regularized activities, themselves have been elaborated and extended through the genres of communication that have become part of their constitution. Thus the activity of law depends on law libraries that contain legislation, commentaries, precedents, and legal journals. Each new case involves exchanges of letters, writs, subpoenas, briefs, opinions, and many other kinds of documents. Much of what it means to take legal action consists of reading and writing within specific domains of texts and text circulation. Government too is built on laws and court decisions, as well as bureaucratic regulations, reports, filings, and thousands of other documents—so much so that government has come to be characterized as being about "red tape"—that is, not the heroic commands from a charismatic leader but endless documents, at one time bound in bundles with red tape. Religion, personal counseling, insurance, truck driving and even farming are bound up with literate mediators that play crucial and regular roles within the activity. It has been said, in fact, that the key to successful farming is the keeping of records which allows one to reflect upon one's past practice and plan for the future.

During the European Renaissance printing and increased commerce created greater opportunities for sharing texts with more people across greater social and geographical boundaries. New forms of social, political, cultural, and economic organization proliferated and many new genres arose, speaking to particular needs and audiences, as well as creating markets for their own circulation. These genres were parts of the proliferation of the activities, relationships, and states of consciousness of modernity that the genres themselves in part made possible and brought into being.

Now citizens of all nations live in highly complicated literate worlds of many genres located within many activity and institutional systems that are national and global in scope—which is why ever higher levels of education are required to participate effectively in the institutions and practices of the contemporary world. As we experience the literate world, we come to recognize, almost as second nature, large numbers of genres and the situations that they carry with them. We do so almost unreflectively, responding imaginatively to the worlds they crystallize for us almost as soon as we see them. When we look at the newspaper (whether paper or digital) we immediately recognize stories of disasters or political conflict, as well as financial reports, movie reviews, and sports stories. We read these transparently as representations of each of the domains they report on. We become more consciously aware of genres when we meet new ones, and we need some orientation to what is going on. The first time we receive a particular kind of notice from the government we may understand the words, but we may not understand what offices and regulations are involved, what our responsibilities and obligations are, and what situation and interactions are being initiated. To understand the document we need to understand what is going on and what our part in these events are. Without that understanding we lose our power to see what documentary systems we are being enlisted into and we lose the ability to assert our rights and needs. Being aware of genres and the associate systems helps us identify where we might write back, intervening to advance our own concerns and positions. Genres to help us think about the situation, the audience, what we might want to accomplish through the text, and what might be recognizable forms we may adopt.

CONVENTIONAL FORMS AND INHABITATIONS

Although we often recognize genres by overt features of form and content, genres are more than a series of conventions regulating form and content. As the previous account suggests, they embody understandings of situations, relationships, stances, moods, strategies, appropriate resources, goals and many other elements that define the activity and shape means of accomplishment. Genres are ways of doing things—and as such embody what is to be done and carry traces of the time and place in which such things are done, as well as the motives and actions carried out in those locales.

From the writer's perspective, locating writing within systems of communications, genres, and unfolding situations helps contend with the blank page problem—that is, what we put on the page has no definition until we give it some. Genre helps give purpose and form to what we write, as well as identifies expectations readers are likely to have. Genre may also help us know how our writing fits within historically evolving situations (see Chapter 3) and relates to previously written texts relevant to this activity system (see Chapter 4). Moreover, as the situation and dynamics take over our imagination, we can respond almost viscerally, in the way we respond to the presence of others. In writing a letter to the editor our words may spill out on the page with passion, in writing an apology our embarrassment may be palpable even though no other person is in front of us, and in writing a proposal for a new business we may become increasingly excited by the possibilities we are projecting. As we warm up to writing a letter to a friend, we remember particular experiences we shared, particular ongoing concerns, particular shared projects. As we start to enact the bonds of our friendship and develop an idea we know they will understand, we find the place our communication resides in and we start inhabiting it with what we are moved to transact there.

As we are caught up in the mentally projected situation, we start to create a presence that speaks to the situation. While filling out an application form for a fellowship, we begin to give shape to the self-presentational spot we are on, and craft an account of ourselves to fulfill the criteria the agency has set out, selecting and highlighting particular personal resources we bring to the situation. The genre of application identifies for us a social space and a mandate that we take on if we decide to apply and want to maximize our chances for success. Our general knowledge about the application as a genre of self-presentation and the specific formal requirements of the application (guided by instructions about the kinds of information required with format and length constraints) elicit information from us and direct us to represent ourselves in a particular way. Insofar as we reflect rhetorically on this task, we recognize how we might fulfill this space in ways that will impress ourselves upon the reviewers and enter into their imagination as the kind of person with the kind of project they were looking for. We go beyond the basic requirements of the genre to inhabit it more robustly, distinguishing our application from the others in a way that will help the agency reviewers imagine we would be an excellent choice to receive their support or fill their position.

Each genre is embedded in a system of activity that we recognize and locate ourselves in, but each time we engage with a genre as writer or reader is also a particular moment in our lives, the lives of the respondents we meet over the text, and activity the systems we meet within. In this way the genre is attached to things that are both more extensive and more specific than we may understand the textual form in itself to be. Further, as we locate ourselves in the genred transaction that resides within the larger system, creating the space for a local moment, we are able to enter into the scene imaginatively, flexibly, creatively, and spontaneously, embodying ourselves in that imagined socially-recognizable space.

ACTIVITY SYSTEMS

The recognizable social spaces of genres have developed simultaneously with the activity systems they are part of and that they allow us to participate in. Activity systems are historically emerged networks of people and artifacts (such as buildings, machines, and products, as well as texts and files) that carry out typified kinds of work and other activities over extended periods, and that have developed ways of coordinating the work and attention of participants in ways that become familiar to all participants. That is, to operate successfully within each you have to become aware of their historically emerged way of doing what they do, and to coordinate your actions with those roles, procedures, regulations, and formats that direct activity within each. A game of baseball is an activity system and so is an amateur league which organizes interested players into teams, schedules a season of games, and maintains records of competitive standings of teams and players. While some activity systems are smaller and some are larger, they each coordinate the distributed work of multiple participants by defining roles and forms of action. Some of the activity systems have immediately visible manifestations—you can see baseball players playing at different positions, handling and throwing the ball or attempting to hit it with a bat—in sequences and patterns explicable by a set of familiar rules and strategies, carrying out goals that are definable within the system. But some of the activity systems or their parts are less immediately visible, so that when watching a game you may not be much aware of the league, except perhaps for some paperwork that needs to be filed by the team coach. Yet the two teams would not be likely to show up on the same field at the same time unless a league official had made a schedule.

There are even less visible aspects, carried only by print, words, and records, kept in orderly ways in relation to the less symbolic elements of the activity system. At professional baseball games, fans hold scorecards, and reporters sit up in the press box. The manager in the dugout may have a notebook of statistics to support decisions. Similarly, in hospitals you may see doctors and nurses treating patients, but there are also offices where accounting and insurance records are kept and processed. There is a library with the scientific and technical literature. There are patient records kept at a station in each ward and a clipboard of vital signs at the foot of each bed. Each of the doctors in a personal office has an individual collection of literature and records—and access to more extensive electronic collections—as well as reading that serves to relax and inspirit them in their emotionally and physically draining work.

Some activity systems are so predominantly conceptual and textual that you can understand very little of them by looking at them. Walking through a university building, all you may see are people sitting alone in offices or together in classrooms, looking at books and computer screens or talking with each other. That tells you very little about the activity systems they are engaged in. To understand what is going on in a classroom, you need to understand what discipline it is part of and how the class fits into the course sequences outlined in the university and departmental requirements. Even more immediately, to understand the activity of a particular class you need to know the texts assigned, the schedule of lectures and discussions, reading and writing assignments, and exams. Once you have placed that day's class within all these systems, you might have some hope of understanding why and how that day's class unfolds in the forms it does.

Similarly, if you were to go into the professor's office and ask what he or she is doing staring at a computer screen, if the document is a memo for a faculty committee you may hear about complex bureaucratic procedures, the entire system of university administration and faculty governance, the political struggles between faculty groups, or the current issues that are exercising people. Or if the professor is working on a paper you may hear about the particular scholarly issue at stake and the professor's current research, the specifics of the conferences and journals the work is being prepared for, or the empirical and interpretive practices, argumentative forms, and organization of the literature typical of the professor's discipline. Or if the professor is a in a cynical mood you will hear about the publication requirements for tenure and promotion.

TEXTS WITHIN ACTIVITY SYSTEMS

When you are writing or reading a text, it helps to know where that text fits in which activity system. Such knowledge helps you identify the likely reader or writer, the typical motives and actions at play, the constraints and resources, the stances and expectations. That knowledge may come from your ongoing embedded engagement or it may come from a more conscious analysis of the situation. For example, a student given a question to write on may be so caught up in the on-going discussion of the classroom and readings, she may spontaneously know what she wants to write and the form it needs to take to contribute to the class discussion. The embodied involvement the ongoing activity may have so shaped the writer's consciousness, that what she writes is germane and appropriate as a matter of course—though I have seen many students caught short by the differences between the dynamic of classroom discussion and the demands of a major written assignment. If the assignment asks for something more or different than what spontaneously flows from prior discussion, the student needs to think about both the prior discussion as setting the stage for the assignment and how the assignment changes the stage—by demanding a different kind of statement, by requiring new resources to be brought in, by changing the audience, or simply by shifting from oral to written mode. Even more, if she is confused by an assignment that seems not to flow directly from what has previously happened, it would help her to think about how the question relates to the instructor's goals for the course and expectations for the assignment, how it fits within the total syllabus of the term and the course evaluation system, how it draws on or shifts terms from the prior readings and discussions, and who else might read it from what stance. It also would help her to think about her own participation in the course and what thoughts and interests she has developed that the paper might advance.

For example, in an introductory political theory course, after several major theories have been read, lectured about, and interpreted, the instructor starts asking comparative questions in discussion to help students see how different theories give support to different kinds of governmental activity. The instructor then assigns a paper for students to choose one governmental agency and see how two different theories might suggest different ways of carrying out that function and how they would in turn evaluate the current operations of the relevant government agency. The student might recognize that she is interested in understanding how certain government programs she values can be justified, but she might recognize that so far this term she has only been critical of theories presented. She may then recognize in this paper an opportunity to reconsider the theories examined in the course to find the positive initiatives buried in each—with reference to one program she favors. In short, in seeing the class as an activity system the student can get a completer picture of where her own writing fits in, what kind of piece in what kind of puzzle her own impulses might motivate her to create.

In a different kind of example, someone seeking reimbursement for large medical expenses from a major illness is more likely to be successful if he understands something about the organization of activities and document flows in his health insurance company. He will be helped in making effective decisions about which documents to file at what point using what keywords and how to coordinate with the doctor and hospitals if he understands which office receives his reimbursement forms; how that office relates to the records received from the medical providers; what decisions are made automatically by rules and are perhaps even computerized; how category codes of diagnoses, procedures and expenses might affect the reimbursement decisions; who makes decisions on more complex cases requiring individualized judgments and what information is used at what juncture in the process; how the application winds up in this individualized procedure; and so on, through the many complexities of the insurance company and its relation to health and governmental agencies. The points of intervention then become clearer along with the kinds of information, arguments, and actions that are likely to be effective at each juncture. Of course, ordinary patients usually have very little of such information, and that is why they may need advocates, just as we need advocates (another term for lawyer) to deal with the legal system.

Some activity systems are more tightly or bureaucratically bound than others, involving technical considerations of precise timing and form, while others have greater opportunity for flexible intervention at multiple points in somewhat novel form to accommodate local situations, mobilizing individual motives and resources. For example, journalistic publicity for a charitable organization may be sought in numerous ways. Offering a friendly reporter an interview and photo opportunity for a human-interest story around the

Christmas holidays, letters to the editor, announcements of national prizes, a lecture by a national celebrity—all could also generate positive publicity on the pages of the newspaper.

RECOGNIZING GENRES

As these examples suggest, communications tend to flow within activity systems in typical pathways, at typical moments, in typical forms, to enact typical intentions, carrying out familiar acts. Newspapers carry certain kinds of stories, in relation to events and the calendar, and people who hope to gain presence in the newspapers need to have their concerns reportable in one of the forms that newspapers publish. Students may get to share their developing understanding or views with their instructors, but only in certain formats—exams, papers, class discussions, perhaps individual discussion during office hours, or chance meetings at the campus coffee-bar if the professor is particularly accessible.

These typical actions carrying out stabilized familiar intentions in recognizable textual forms are those things we call genres. Genres are simultaneously categories of textual forms, forms of social interaction, and forms of cognitive recognition and shaping of motive and thought. That is, when a text suddenly appears before our eyes, comes to our desk, or arrives in our mailbox, we start categorizing it on the basis of certain textual features. It appears on a certain kind of paper—cheap newsprint folded into about twenty double-size, double-sided pages or a single sheet of plain white 81/2 X 11 office paper. It may have a generic heading—"memo" or "proposal"—or the name of a familiar newspaper. From this we start to form expectations of what it will contain, the kind of people it is from, what kind of relationship the writer has to us, what kind of stance the writer will take, how the parts should be arranged, where we should look for specific material, and most importantly why we would or would not be interested in it and what we would do with it. In short, we start to frame personal meaningfulness for our personal purposes and interactions.

We also form expectations and hypotheses about the document based on when and where it comes to us and our knowledge about the senders and our relationship to us. It is delivered to the doorstep of our home in the morning. It comes in the mail with a return address of a bank with which we have no current business. It arrives in our office inbox signed by the name of the CEO of our company. Large areas of our social knowledge are activated to work in tandem with what we find in the text to help us identify what the text is about and what kind of attention we might give it. Thus we enter into a mental conception of a social space for interaction within which we start to build relevant meanings, evaluations, and stances. In recognizing the genre, we locate an orientation toward the text and the details we will find inscribed within it.

If there are gross violations of the expected interaction—if the CEO starts telling intimate confessions about his personal life, if the bank with which we do not do business sends us a statement of our account, if the newspaper has advanced physics equations on its front page—we may well wonder about what is going on. We wonder whether our boss's psychological life is in disarray, or we are a target of a financial fraud. On the other hand, we may find the answer in the way writers are deploying multiple and complex understandings of discourse to accomplish novel purposes in the documents. The CEO who regularly sends out messages to build support for his leadership may, when facing a scandal, attempt to maintain support by invoking genres of confession and contrition by baring his heart in the public space of the memo. The bank may be advertising through fictionalized projected statements of wealth if you were to take advantage of their services. The newspaper in attempting to report a major breakthrough may want to quote physical equations not so you can make calculations, but so you may look in wonder that such a strange phenomenon may be explained by such a simple equation. Multiple generic expectations are being combined in creative ways to evoke special meanings for each specific situation.

PERSONAL AND PUBLIC HISTORIES WITH GENRES

We learn about what to expect from genres through public and personal histories of experience with them. Similar looking documents have circulated in similar systems, available to many participants over a period of time, so that a range of people can come to recognize and orient toward these documents with similar understandings of what the documents are doing. Thus the writers can create similar texts with a reasonable expectation that those understandings will be evoked by the documents, particularly if the text is given all the physical appearances that make it recognizable as an exemplar of the genre. At the same time, our own repertoire of generic understandings is also a function of our personal experiences with these publicly available genres. Before beginning to work as a paralegal, we may have very limited sense of the documents that typically circulate in the legal system, but within a fairly rapid time by observing, and asking questions we can start to get a sense of the kinds of documents we need to work with. Additionally, prior experiences may make us familiar with a special repertoire we may recognize in a more refined way than our co-workers. If, for example, before working for a law firm we previously worked in an insurance company, we might be specially skilled in understanding internal insurance company documents when they surface in the course of litigation.

Some genres are well known to almost all members of a culture and are identifiable by name—for examples in contemporary U.S. cultures most people are aware of personal thank you letters, autobiographical narratives, and newspaper editorials. Each of these genres is frequently taught in the middle grades of schooling, thereby assuring wide familiarity. But in those areas where we have special experience we may have a very refined set of generic recognitions, some of which we may articulate with names shared with other experts, but some may be entirely private recognitions. For example, auto insurance examiners may know that within the standard damage reports, reports of some kinds of typical damage from typical accidents don't need very much elaboration beyond a few stock phrases and reference to standard book values. However, if a custom car is involved there may be needed more extensive, novel narrative of damage and needed repair. Such special contingencies and situations might suggest to an experienced examiner various kinds of information and narratives that would meet the needs of the insurance company and address potential litigation. Some of these additional reports may be laid out in requirements, but some of them may simply be known through experience of many cases and reading many examples. Some variants may be entirely idiosyncratic and lack names as when an examiner over the years has learned that when he writes up certain kinds of cases in a certain way he runs into difficulties, but if he writes them up in slightly different way, they are never questioned. Similarly, in reading reports, he may sense that some of them give him a slightly funny feeling that tell him he needs to check out a particular aspect of the case, but these have no general public name and general recognizability.

There is no limit to the number of genres, nor can we say the term refers to document types of any generality, size, or level of public recognizability. The process of genre recognition occurs any time any person at any level of awareness makes some differentiation or particularization of texts on the basis of kind. Of course, it would be foolish in writing a document to a wide audience to rely on all the readers being familiar with an esoteric or personally idiosyncratic genre. On the other hand, if personal knowledge of that genre helps you frame a solution to a rhetorical problem that can be understood or interpreted in a more general way, then that unusual genre knowledge has served you well. A rock composer may use detailed knowledge of Bach's three-part inventions to provide harmonic richness to a song, which is hearable to most listeners simply as a love song with a bit of a classical sound. On the other hand, certain listeners of the same song may recognize the ironic invocation of folk gospel protest songs signaled by hortatory metaphoric lyrics, but set against the self-absorption of teenage love ballads of the nineteen fifties backed by syrupy fake-classical orchestrations. One of the traditional roles of literary and artistic criticism has been, indeed, to unpack the complex play of types evoked by artistic works that achieve novel and complex effects.

WHAT DO WE LEARN FROM EXPERIENCE WITH GENRES?

Through experience we learn about types of utterances that occur within certain types of circumstances, so that we become attuned to recognize them. Through experience we learn much about how those utterances go, how we might understand them, what makes them succeed and fail, and what their consequences might be. The first time we may need to write a letter of recommendation for a co-worker seeking a new job, we may be uncertain about the best things to write and how to present them. But as we come to read and write many such letters, we gain an extensive repertoire of strategies and elaborations to draw on, depending on her personal characteristics and accomplishments, the nature of the job she is applying for, and the particular situation and process of hiring, We also know what has captured our attention when reading such letters and what we have found implausible or irrelevant. We know what kinds of letters have helped people get jobs and which are ignored. This detailed strategic knowledge can be at any level of the rhetorical and linguistic realization—from what typeface looks authoritative and what phrases provide a sense of spontaneous authenticity, to what kind of details establish the depth of knowledge of the applicant. We not only know the genre, we know what we can say through the genre, and how the genre can be made to work.

Even more with experience working with the genre we become familiar with the variation of situations in which it can be used and the ways the genre can serve to transform or evolve any particular situation. If we know something about the organizations our friend is seeking work at, we can modify the letter to fit the particular hiring processes of the company, the corporate culture, their current needs, and what they look for in job candidates; we can particularize the presentation to fit the situation.

GENRES AS A FRAME FOR READING AND WRITING

Genres frame and locate the moment of writing, but do not obscure it within generalities. The genre identifies, we might say, a room and an event, and implies some orientations, typical understandings, tools, and possible trajectories, but it does not tell us exactly how the event is going to unfold. That is up to the actual people working through their own particular interests and modes of existence in their own particular ways as they make the event real and particular. The act of writing then realizes the potentials of action in the generically shaped moment, a way of fulfilling intentions and goals that can be achieved within the genre.

If the generic space is crisply defined and compulsory at the moment, and we have visited such a space often, we enter the genre's habitat like a well-trained and well-prepared actor enters into a familiar role, with one's entire body and emotions, yet with a reflective distance because we know exactly what the role is and how to enact it. We can look at the drama unfolding even as we are totally within it. We may have written shopping lists a thousand times and have well developed procedures for searching the larder and projecting the week's food needs and menus of upcoming parties—nonetheless, we are still thoroughly within the activity of producing that shopping list, surveying the stale food in the refrigerator, uncertain about whether the milk is enough to get us through to next shopping without running out or going sour, and anxious about the dinner party that evening.

If the generic space is complex and unfamiliar, on the other hand, too much may be at play to see clearly where all our understandings, thoughts, and impulses are leading us; nonetheless, even fragmented understanding of the generic demands and possibilities of the emerging situation can help to direct and focus our confusions—it is a habitat that we can begin to recognize. As we recognize that the endangered community day care needs to gather the support of several key members of the City Council, and that each might be reached in a different way—one by narratives and personal testimony about the difference the center has made for local women, another by a detailed economic report of how the center has extended the work force of local small businesses, another by the personal evaluation of a long-time respected advisor, another by a description of the educational character of the children's activities—we start to get a better sense of what we are doing, and where we need to go to reach our long term goals. We may not be sure we understand exactly what is happening and how well our words are meeting the situation, but we can start to gather thoughts and channel energies into specific rhetorical tasks.

In either case, whether familiar and simple or unfamiliar and complex, this habitat becomes a space in which we start to have spontaneous thoughts in reaction to the particulars of the situation brought together in the interactive space. With the shopping list, as we remember we will have a vegetarian guest tonight, we realize we will need to improvise a dish using a tofu substitute for the meat, and as we see more eggs in the refrigerator than expected, we may start to list other ingredients for the omelets that have just entered into the menu. Similarly, as we discover that the niece of a council member lives in the area served by the day care and sends her child there, we may think of inviting the niece to testify, but realizing that might seem too heavy-handed, we decide to ask women in situations similar to the niece to testify, perhaps even women the niece knows.

Thus as the situation emerges in the genred habitats, we come to populate it with the specifics of life that are far from rule determined or faceless. Even the simplest and most recurrent spaces can become complex and novel.

RECOGNIZABLE ASPECTS OF GENRE

Often people associate genres with specific textual features or conventions that signal presence of the genre or with particular textual patterns or constraints that come into play once you are in a genre. The genre of sonnet is constitutive of a formal kind of poem, regulated in formal features of number of lines, verse and rhyme patterns, meter, and (somewhat more flexibly) subject and stance. Patent applications are legally regulated in the content and by tradition and practice in some of their formal appearances. On the other hand, textbooks of different subjects, levels, and pedagogic philosophies and strategies may vary in formal appearances, but what is characteristic of them all is that the books are designed to fit into classroom practices.

Certainly some genres are highly regulated with many compulsory features. On income tax returns the taxpayer is highly compelled in what he or she must fill in on each line—name, total gross income, and so on. Even the specific answer is held accountable by many procedures and related documents so that the taxpayer cannot make up any number to place in the gross income space. A letter complaining about a product and seeking refund also must do a number of standard things to accomplish its ends: identify the product, the place and time of purchase, the defect, the warranty conditions, the address and identity of the writer, the specific required adjustment. Further, the letter of complaint is more likely of success if it follows a standard format of business letters. Yet a personal letter to a friend who works for a small company may accomplish the task without once breaking into formality, though it still requires all the necessary information. The friend will recognize the business letter that lies beneath and within the friendly note. On the other hand, a business letter that has all the formal markings and overt signs may fail because it is directed toward the wrong officer in the company. The company may in fact have intentionally made it confusing to figure out who an unhappy customer should send the letter to as a way to evade responsibility.

Similarly, the opening phrase "Once upon a time, long ago . . ." signals many literary understandings about the text drawing on our familiarity with the genre of fairy tale. Yet such signaling hardly encompasses all we come to understand about a genre. Although a story may start out the path of a fairy tale, it may immediately overlay that with science fiction, as in the opening of the movie *Star Wars*— "Once upon a time, long ago, in a galaxy far away . . ." Many kinds of understandings are subsequently invoked as the movie creates its own place out of many worlds of literary narrative.

Given this range of features that may signal a genre and the range of aspects that might be then considered typical or constitutive of the genre, the best way to come to understand a genre is descriptive rather than by any prescriptive definition of necessary features. What features to describe as most characteristic of the genre cannot be determined outside of human use and practice. Rather we as analysts might best begin with what seems to form the similarity and what other people seem to orient toward in talking about similarity. We might consider what would surprise the genre users within the genre and how they would recognize the difference between neighboring similar genres. We should note what aspects of the genre clue the users into its nature, and what kind of assumptions or attitude they take for granted as part of the genre. We might then note what kinds of thoughts users mobilize when they recognize the genre, and what kinds of interactions they sense they are entering into with what kind of partners in what kind of institutional setting, in what situation and moment. That is, we need to take seriously the idea that genre is a psycho-social recognition category and not fixed in the form of the text. We should rather attempt to characterize what triggers the recognition and what users then recognize.

GENRES AS A POTENTIAL SPACE OF READING AND ITS TROUBLES

It is one thing to recognize a potential place of discursive activity within some ongoing interaction and activity system and even to start to construct an utterance that would start to carry forward the activity. It is quite another as writers to have our desired co-participants meet us in that place, to attend to the discourse at all, let alone with shared understanding. To put it bluntly, we cannot always get our desired readers to read what we have written, nor with the desired level of attention, nor with the spirit and attitude we hope for. They may not want to come into the room we create, or at least through the door we hoped, and they may not remain long enough to understand in detail what we want to show them. On the other hand, they may stay around too long, poking into corners and under rugs we don't care to have them looking into.

We may write a poem and nobody will come visit it. Articles for publication have to be inviting enough and of the right sort for the editors and reviewers of the journal to grant space to reach the readers of the journal or magazine or newspaper. Even if our text gets published, it does not mean that readers will find the title and subject sufficiently inviting to do more than rush by the door, or step in for a quick look and then wander away. So the realization of the genre needs to come alive and deliver something of value to the readers who drop by with some expectations. It needs to be an attractive example of the genre— but what makes attractiveness may be very particular to the genre and to the specific case. In reports of stocks, signs of timeliness and accuracy and depth of judgment may convince investors to spend their time reading further. Readers of celebrity fan stories, however, may be looking for endearing personal details.

On the other hand, sometimes people are obligated within their activity system to attend to a text. Tax inspectors are bound by their conditions of employment to look over tax forms, and every U.S. income tax form now undergoes a preliminary computer inspection. So although we don't desire a close reading of those texts, we know there will be at least a certain level of reading, matching numbers on various filings. In fact one rhetorical aim we may have in filling out our forms is to fill out the form so as to not invite a deeper reading that might be triggered by some claims that would make the filing "interesting" or "suspect." That is we want a certain level of reading and no more. There are many situations, surprisingly, where we desire to satisfy a certain level of reading without inviting any deeper or different sets of reading. We might want our comments on a political candidate to be read as a common-sense evaluation of their character and accomplishments, without invoking the sense that we may be speaking from an ideological or partisan position. We may want to write a letter to a friend attempting to heal a bond without invoking the differences that caused the problem; we want the letter to be read as a gesture of pure friendship rather than as a continuing justification of our actions. We may want the reader of our historical essay to understand the narrative we construct out of the archival material, but not to question our archival methods; we may even make some statements indicating our standard professional technique so as to block that kind of suspicious reading. We want to control the multiplicity of reading such generic recognitions might invoke.

In some other circumstances, however, we might want to move the reader beyond an ordinary reading to another level. Students writing a paper for an instructor usually want to write the essay to fit the generic expectations of the assignment to avoid a failing grade. However, some students may wish to do more than meet the generic requirements of the assignment to be judged acceptable or even receive an A—they seek to share their thinking and to engage the teacher in dialogue as a fellow intellectual or a personal mentor.

How others will take up our comments is ultimately beyond our control—there are limits to how much we can compel others to attend to our words and what kinds of interpretations they may pursue. Yet it is worth considering how to encourage readers to take up an invitation and how to keep them from seeing the text as an opportunity for quarrels and other unwanted interactions. This issue is explored more fully in Chapter 7 of the accompanying volume on the Interaction Order.

SO WHERE ARE WE? HAVE WE LEFT THE MATERIAL WORLD BEHIND?

Having created a recognizable social discursive space for interaction within an activity system, and having made it inviting enough for others to join in the party—where does this party take place in relation to the daily, embodied world in which we live surrounded by other people, weather, animals, rocks, and buildings? Although we may meet people in the mental spaces created by genres, both writers and readers live in material social worlds of here and now (although the here and now of each may be quite distinct). If these texts influence people, we might reasonably assume they influence how people walk around and greet people in the material world—or do they live, as Auden claims of poetry, in the "valley where nothing happens"?

Some genres are directly operative within activity systems that move bodies and objects around. Shipment orders, bills of lading, and signable receipts put people and goods in trucks and hold the people accountable for delivering the goods to other people at certain times. Paperwork in numerous genres makes possible our system of transfer and movement of goods. In a corporation, each of the departments—production, sales, marketing, management, and legal—adds its own layers of paperwork to facilitate making goods and profits and holding personnel accountable to planned and monitored activities.

As police officers are often heard to complain, the apprehension, trial, conviction, incarceration, and even execution of criminals is surrounded by unending genres of paperwork. Despite the claims that this paperwork keeps the police and other law enforcers from doing their work, it is precisely this paperwork that ensures law enforcement is the work, rather than an unrestrained and unaccountable exercise of state violence. These law enforcement genres certainly move bodies around, but in so doing have the potential of transforming those movements into a rule of law and bureaucratic efficiency—although not always consistently achieved. The inscriptions created within these genres then influence the status and life possibilities of each individual inscribed within that activity system—incarcerated felon or upstanding citizen.

People who work in such systems have some, though perhaps grumbling, knowledge of the values of the genres in their field. Some of the grumbling, in fact, may come from the participants knowing only too well how such documents make their actions and choices accountable. Making an account is the essence of making oneself accountable. In any event, people could not knowledgably and intelligently complete the various genres they are required to complete without some understanding of how these documents circulate and with what effect. A regular form of training in police and similar organizations is to raise neophytes' understanding of the consequences of the documents they create, so that they take them seriously and provide the kinds of information necessary for the operations of the rest of the activity system. The more nurses and doctors understand the kinds of things that can happen if they do not accurately update the patient's chart, the more they are likely to write what is likely to be needed.

Through such activity systems, not only are the material and bodily movements regulated, they are given meanings. Controlled violence becomes law and order. Buildings are built that in turn control the movement of people through halls and elevators and provide locales for interaction. But these buildings also become part of an educational or a corporate plan or an urban design. They are even given ideological meaning and consequences as classrooms are built on an open design or prisons built with panoptical effectiveness.

Educational research on the effectiveness of various arrangements of the classroom and penology research on the controllability and/or rehabilitative effectiveness of prison designs in turn may influence architectural documents which will then influence the future environments that people will live in. Studies in the sociology and psychology of education may influence arrangement of seating and the presence of various learning artifacts. Even more, ideas and research may transform people's self-understanding of what they are doing in situations, thereby influencing their behavior. Teachers may talk to students differently, gather them in different groupings, assign them different activities, provide different kinds of feedback and support on the basis of the research and theory that makes its way to teacher education programs, curricular designers, textbook makers, and individual teachers.

The genres of psychiatric theory, research, and taxonomies of disorders influence how clinicians interact with people who seek help and what categories they provide for patients' self-understanding. These texts influence what therapies are offered, what the precise course of treatment looks like, and the behavioral and emotional criteria by which clients and treatments will be evaluated. They also influence whom insurance companies will reimburse for what kinds of treatment. Through such means, the abstract work of psychological theory becomes embodied in peoples' lives.

Even the seemingly unworldly activity systems of literature can be traced back to middle-class people sitting in easy chairs during leisure hours, contemplating their lives, seeking extensions of their experience vicariously, or escaping daily woes by exercising fantasies. This is not even to speak of the entire industry and economics of literary publication, print, book sales, and cultural marketing that keep many people and objects on the move.

Genres are also held accountable in their own ways to embodied life, social activity, and other realms outside their boundaries. To carry out their work properly and without excessive failure producers of genred texts need to attend to the kinds of realities they inscribe and the kinds of realities that might catch them up short. Within a rule of law, police must have just cause and evidence for their actions, which they must be able to produce in courts and other sites of accountability. If they cannot produce the blood samples and ballistic tests that match the criminal to the crime, their work adds up to little and they may even lose public support. Excessive numbers of patient mortalities may lead regulators and the public to call into question hospital records that indicate no dire problem. A collapsed bridge calls into account all the reports, plans, contracts, and inspection reports that went into its construction and maintenance.

Newspapers are regularly evaluated by the readers and critics on the procedures by which they gather their stories and their care in substantiation. Professional journalists develop their standards of ethics by which they hold themselves accountable precisely so as to raise the public estimation of their work. Newspapers as well are held accountable by competition from other papers and news media, by interest groups and politicians trying to tell their side of the story, by courts and laws, and ultimately by historians. None of these processes creates an absolute accountability, but rather each provides a specific kind of challenge that will draw on different evidence, arguments, and questioning strategies. The newspapers must be able to adequately answer such challenges from all these directions by the way they gather news (so as to consider the positions of opposite sides, so as to avoid malicious slander, so as to dig out facts faster than the competition and not to have been blatantly mistaken, so as in the long run to appear as a reasonable source for history, etc.).

Knowledge producing disciplines, similarly, each have procedures for holding its members accountable to evidence and experiences that are drawn on. In anticipation of being called into account, researchers will gather and inscribe evidence according to the accepted methods and standards of the field. Skeptical readers or readers of different experience, findings, and conviction may well demand an accounting or be able to provide persuasive contrary evidence. However, these forms of developing accountable evidence vary with the disciplines—gaining a sample of current dialect use through interview with a person deemed a local speaker and transcribing the recording according to current linguistic conventions has a very different relation to the material world than drilling a geologic core and running the components through a variety of chemical analytic tests. Each must then defend itself against different sorts of skeptical questions.

DISPLAYING THE MATERIAL CONDITIONS OF TEXTS' CREATION AND USE

Some texts overtly remind readers of the physical location of their purported creation, ("As I sit here in my prison cell considering the political conditions that . . ."; "This study was set in motion by certain practical problems regularly confronted by all teachers. . . ."; "I write this letter much agitated upon hearing of your impending risky venture . . ."), of the text's imagined circulation ("As this plea reaches out to people in all lands . . ."; "In the several days this letter takes to reach you . . ."), or of conditions of reception and use of this text ("Heed these words wisely as you set off in your adventures in car maintenance.") Texts often use an imaginative reconstruction of these sites of material writing, publication, and reading as tropes in their own arguments. Some genres even specify that conditions of production or use be represented within the texts to serve specific rhetorical functions, as the experimental report requires an account of the initiating scientific problem; of the method carried out in the laboratory; and of the actual laboratory happenings—all of which established the conditions and material for the writing of the report. Similarly, institutional reports often require accounts of the initiating problem and the procedures by which the report was produced. On the other end, some genres explicitly index the conditions of reading and use. For example, repair manuals for physical devices direct you toward locations and procedures to be immediately found on the object: "Note on the left front panel, just beneath the display labeled 'distortion' is a circular dial. As you turn this dial clockwise, when the indicator line passes the vertical position, you will notice a slight, brief click. This click enables you to locate the base position."

Even without these explicit indicators, however, each text has specific conditions of production, circulation, and use. Our perception of these conditions influences our understanding of the character and force of the text. In writing the text we usually are only too aware of the conditions we write under—our limited resources, our wandering attention, our slightly chilly room, our boss breathing down our neck. But at the same time those conditions are transformed by the ideological and social nature of the genre. We may be sitting at our desk, but that desk is enlisted into a hierarchical and competitive world of corporate activity, into an evaluative world of an academic course we are taking, or into the communal work of encouraging friends who are starting an environmental organization.

Our texts are shaped by the social ideological worlds they are produced for, and those same worlds are likely to define the distribution and circulation of the texts. The corporate document is cycled up the organization, to be transformed by managers who combine it with information from other documents, to be used in particular meetings as a warrant for further actions. The classroom essay is placed on the professor's desk to be marked and returned. The access of other people to that classroom assignment will be limited unless the professor spells out particular procedures of group work or publication as part of the educational experience of the class. The shopping list accompanies us to the supermarket and then winds up in the wastebasket.

The conditions of use are equally generically shaped by the documents that help shape them. The corporate memo is to be read by a subordinate to identify the procedures for carrying out an assignment. Another researcher reads our research reports as part of a literature search while contemplating a new research project, or assigns it to a graduate seminar for them to learn the literature of the field. Within each of these concrete settings, the documents we write add particular meanings, representations, and actions to carry the activities along. Through filling virtual spaces of interaction by our written genres we create meanings that influence others. Our texts become social facts in their worlds, creating acts out of language. Rhetoric is the art of understanding how that creation of meaning works, so we a can make meanings that work better for human action.

CHAPTER 3
WHEN YOU ARE

Time as well as space creates problems for texts. Although texts are written at a point in time (or, more exactly, over a span of time, which has an end point at which the texts are considered adequate to be presented to the intended audience) and they are read at another moment (or again, more exactly, a finite span of time), those moments may be far apart and have little to do with each other except for the text that binds them together. Just as pieces of paper may appear to be tied down to no particular place, they seem attached to no particular time. The textual artifact can endure for years without being used or even looked at. While texts from the future are still a matter of science fiction, any text still surviving from the past is available for our current use. Nonetheless, texts arise from historical moments in situations, are directed toward others located in historical moments, with specific intent to accomplish ends—influencing people and events within history. So where and how do we locate texts in time?

In a large scale way we can see the temporality of texts in the changes of genres that give them shape and locate them within activity systems. Texts seen as being in older genres carry the scent of a world whose time has passed. Texts also date in more specific ways. The specific occasions which give rise to texts emerge, coalesce, then evaporate; or change; or become ossified to become curious historical landmarks that constrain a changing world. The specific occasions of reading may be also be concretely tied to immediate events, as one may refer to a weather prediction the evening before heading out on a fishing trip, but the weather prediction past its time is not much use, unless to settle a barroom bet by corroborating an elaborate fish story.

When long-standing texts are seen as still current in their force and meaning, they tend to maintain earlier moments and arrangements within changing circumstances, such as happens with sacred texts, constitutions, or (more obviously problematically) anachronistic laws. Usually the relevance and force of such enduring texts are supported by equally enduring cultural and social institutions and practices, such as schools, churches, and courts. Even if our attentions remain fixed on a long-lived historical text supported by enduring social institutions, changing events and contexts bring temporal mutability to the reading and thus the interpretation and meaning of the texts, such as the extensive theological arguments among religious sects and constitutional divisions among legal scholars attempting to determine an absolute meaning of a text from long ago. The attention of readers and the sense they may make of the text change and evaporate as time and conditions move on, so no ossification can be absolute. More typically, when we read texts out of their specific cultural and activity time, we too are engaged in new activities at our moment. Our current concerns may lead previously ignored documents to suddenly become newly significant, warranting detailed reexamination. Literary history is filled with the rising and falling stock of different writers arising from changing cultural concerns and tastes. To read through the history of Shakespeare criticism is to learn as much about the obsessions of different cultural moments as it is to learn about Shakespeare. This is equally true of our changing views of political documents and philosophic texts.

These waves of history are what the Greeks called *kairos*, a term that finds its etymology both in an archery target made by stretched strings and the transient openings in the weaving of cloth as the shuttle passes through the emerging network of thread (Miller, 1992, p. 313). This etymology vividly highlights the transience of events and the opportunities and threats events offer, but even more how reacting to those opportunities and threats adds to the unfolding events, helps extend the cloth. Events are moments of cultural formation, of intersubjective attention, and of conjoint activity. Events are phenomenologically perceived by participants as salient in the organization of unfolding activity. In face-to-face conversation time seems to happen unremarkably. We all know the time of day and year, the *chronos* by which we have come to mark time as a regular periodicity. If we are uncertain we can check our watches and calendars or the sun (although calendars and clocks, we should note are inventions precisely to inscribe time in a regularized symbolic order, to be laid on top of unfolding events so we can plan, contemplate, hold each other accountable for timeliness. Less determinatively, however, we also sense the unfolding of events, the phenomenological time we move through in the presence of others—we estimate our days through the pace of the activities we are part of, and in the gathering of people and actions in focused events. At times this sense of the moment comes to conscious attention, such as when we await the right moment to enter into a discussion. Raising to conscious contemplation this sense of the right moment is the function of the classical term of *kairos*, to help us attend to the temporal location, moments that gather and fade, the passing opportunities we may perceive and grab, so as to change the course of events through our timely intervention.

As writers of texts we also ride the waves of time, time in which we perceive our own urgencies of action, time in which we see others pursuing their own course of interests with actions at their own pace. At some moment we perceive events coming together in a time where a text would serve us well.

Our perception of the moment includes whether the time is ripe for other participants to receive our text. Will they pay attention to it? Will it change the course of their actions? Will it redefine a situation for others so that they will receive another person's message differently. By inserting our texts in the right moment in the right situation, we not only assert ourselves, we assert our perception of time and events into the unfolding realities. If others recognize the moment and space of our utterance, they share with us a common moment, a common time of coordinated attention. The recognition of genre is important in this coordination. Insofar as we create a mutually recognizable act in such shared moments, we create a social fact that may have long-term consequences for us and the others who come after. In writing we need to shoot an arrow from our time to land within the time net of others.

In our texts we even create further senses of time. The text is something that is read within time, and has its own pace or affords the reader multiple options of time in reading. We may write a text that needs slow word-by-word attention if it is to be meaningful or we may design a text that allows a busy executive to find a significant fact rapidly. We may write a text that allows various readers to enter in with different sequence and pacing. We both mesh with their time and then ensnare the reader within the time and space of our text for as long as they stay engaged with our text. This phenomenological sense of textual time transforms the embodied reader's perceived path through the day into a space of information, reflection, and ideational comment, moving with the pace of the ideas held up for inspection in the text. Readers may then return to their embodied world carrying the remnants of the textual time, such as with a panicked sense of rapidly unfolding global climate catastrophe presented in the environmental report the have just read or with the contemplative sense of eternity in a poem. Reading takes time out from the embodied day to assert new time scales and events into it.

One further sense of time in the text is that of the events represented in the text. Our slowly-read text may nonetheless represent a rapidly moving world—a world that we vainly try to hold still by our acts of aesthetic lengthening. Or we may present a world of deep causality where paleolithic events still leave their mark on the current landscape around us. This world of represented time also may change the reader's perception of the embodied world around them. We may walk down the street thinking not only of the ripening season, but of the ripening economy, the ripening of philosophic questions, the geologic unfolding of our region, or the seasons of the heart. So texts are not just themselves part of cultural and historic moments, they influence the experience of moments and the reflective perception of moments. To know the moments of the texts we receive and shape the texts to create moments of attention, spots of time, we need to start to construct a sense of the way texts sit within and locate themselves in time.

WRITING AND THE HISTORY OF CULTURAL MOMENTS

Anyone who has done historical work in archives of a previous century knows how the documents carry the aroma of an earlier way of life. A look at old family documents brings us back not only to past events, but to the pace and relations of past days. Even genres that seem to have a fairly fixed form over time depend on the enduring cultural activity systems in which they reside and thrive, even as these systems evolve. People read novels of a few centuries ago and from another culture, but only because of continuing institutions of leisure, access, and education. Except for a limited number of titles that are continuingly renewed by new editions and film remakes, these older texts vanish into the obscurity of libraries, to be only occasionally looked at by scholars or people with antiquarian tastes—people who as part of their own current activity seek to be transported backward. Jane Austen's novels may be constantly revived, but what about those of contemporary author Tobias Smollett of *Peregrine Pickle* fame, and even lesser literary lights of late eighteenth century England? The revivals of old texts in addition to reinserting those texts within current systems of text distribution and the economics of publication, update the pleasures, and renew and reinterpret tastes and cultural systems of prior dates, holding them up for our own uses of cultural ideals and nostalgia. They also in part reproduce prior structures of cultural consumption, as a culturally complex form of connoisseurship. People delight in being able to spend their leisure by going backwards in imagined time—not only in the subject matter, but in the style of reading.

More concretely, consider such apparently timeless documents as birth and death records. These are only maintained as continuous and accessible by the continuing institutions that collect and house them, such as churches and governments. Even then, as anyone who has worked with such historical records knows, they must be interpreted in terms of the practices and uses of document at the time of original collection. Were births recorded on the first day of life or at baptism or after a year survival, at the hospital, the city hall or a religious institution, of all people or only of certain segments of the population? Further, we only go back to inspect such documentary remains as part of our own current cultural activities, whether reconstructing economic and health conditions or recovering our family histories which carry meanings for us now. Old texts are occasionally revived and given new social meanings by changing social concerns that give them new relevance—currently in the Americas early Spanish colonial documents are being dusted off because of our need to reevaluate colonialism and its impact on a world now trying to reach toward new forms of global organization. Similarly, continuing relevance of ancient legal documents may be affected by the continuity of legal systems that provides such prior documents current legal force or influence.

The continuing relevance of the most ancient and stable of texts, the sacred scriptures of living religions—the Bible, the Mahabharata, the Koran—again depend on the continuing religious institutions wherein they remain centerpieces of moral and philosophic worlds. Scriptural religions revive the texts, constantly reinserting them in people's lives. Similar texts of now extinct religions—such as the Egyptian Book of the Dead—have a different kind of contemporary status, primarily in the activities of scholars or those seeking after hidden knowledge of the ancients. If, however, they should become the center of a renewed cult or are taught in surveys of world culture, they again take on new sets of meanings and new forms of circulation—such as, for example, occurred when the tablets containing the Gilgamesh epic were discovered in 1853 after remaining buried and unread for millennia.

However, even the most stable of sacred scriptures are parts of changing religions in changing worlds, and thus change their meanings. Changing congregations, liturgies, sermonic practices, philosophies, life problems, church economics, and ambient cultural practices—among many other factors—constantly reposition the ancient sacred texts within modern activity systems. Even the most conservative text-bound cults within those religions, most dedicated to maintaining the word as written, nonetheless, constantly change, even just in addressing the contemporary challenges facing them in their efforts to hold to the old ways. It is very different to be a literalist New Testament believer in seventeenth century England than in twenty-first century Georgia or Mexico City.

WRITING AND ACTION MOMENTS

Texts are often part of local and immediate events as these events unfold. For example, an annual projection of a city's economy made by an economist in the employ of the chamber of commerce enables local government and business to plan and make decisions over the ensuing months. One year the release of a particularly dire forecast leads to a series of newspaper stories and statements by local leaders—followed by a plan issued by the local chamber of commerce to be placed before the city council. Each of these documents is timely, speaking to the unfolding events. If a local industry seeks to use these events to gain tax abatement for a long planned expansion, they might time their request for tax relief to take best advantage of the increasing anxiety and to fit into the emerging plan for city action. While all the projections and plans may later be of historical and comparative interest (to answer such currently-oriented questions as how the economy has grown over the years, and what we can learn from responses to previous downturns), they are all in the initial moment directed at influencing actions to be taken in the near term.

Some documents are, however, designed to be used in a variety of situations that may occur over an extended period, such as a reference book like a dictionary. But even then each use is motivated by the particular circumstance and needs of the user, which a well-designed reference attempts to anticipate. What kinds of occasion will send people to a dictionary to check spellings or an alternative meaning? How can the dictionary be designed to be handy for these situations? Even general purpose dictionaries make assumptions about the level of detail and needs of the users, as well as how the users have to configure their behavior to be efficient or appropriate users—in fact we have to be taught in school appropriate and efficient methods of dictionary use.

INDIVIDUAL AND GROUP PERCEPTION OF MOMENTS

The constantly emergent and self-making aspects of *kairos* suggest we need to attend to the unfolding events in which we are engaged, and to notice the process of their unfolding so as to spot targets for our comments. But of course our spotting of openings is influenced by our perceptions, of what is unfolding and where things are going, of what kind of cloth is being woven, and what kind of yarn we may add to make it something that contains our own meanings and desires.

Some targets are clearly held up by others for us to notice as when a funding agency sends us a form that we are invited to complete or a company announces it is accepting employment applications. Our decision is only whether we will aim for those targets. Some of those targets we are even compelled by law to address, as when we are required to submit our annual tax returns or to report births and deaths. Even these communicative moments, however, we may turn our backs on, though at the risk of penalties.

Other targets are so fleeting and evanescent that they only exist when a visionary individual sees it and then speaks to it, providing the means in retrospect by others to recognize the moment that has been seized. Nobody else might have recognized that moment in that way nor seen it as an opportunity to be seized. Imagine a group of people sitting in a circle talking. Each sees different moments to jump in, and each seems to jump in from a different angle, taking the conversation in a particular direction. If it is a particularly heated discussion perhaps several people will always be ready to jump in, as they each note a break in the previous person's talk, a moment at which they might interrupt. However, it is likely that each of these would-be speakers would want to contribute something different. They will each likely find in the discussion to that point a different and will each find a different opening in the moment for weaving a different kind of cloth.

Now extrapolate this situation from face-to-face conversation to communication at a distance. So many documents may be seen by individuals pursuing different sets of interests, that people may likely see the unfolding events and the moments for opportune intervention differently. The resulting texts in response will likely vary in how they represent the moment, what they say, and how they try to seize the moment. Even when many people, aligned in similar ways, are paying attention to widely known events, their senses of the moment may be varied and inchoate until a single text—a government report, the carefully composed speech of a political leader, the powerful sermon— crystallizes a mood and moment. Shared institutions, shared immediate public facts and events, shared social positions and urgencies, then make these audiences ready to accept the author's framing of the moment, letting them recognize through the utterance that this is exactly where they are at and what they need at this moment. No matter how much the speaker's situation is prepared by institutional and historical pressures creating an opportunity, it is only the rhetor's grabbing of the moment in a particular way that coalesces the moment and gives the audience the occasion to recognize what a powerful moment it is.

TYPICAL ACTION SEQUENCES

Even if our words are not part of dramatic one-time events, we often know when in a typical chronological sequence texts come to us and when we need to produce texts in response. Some texts are set according to chronological guidelines. Income taxes in the United States are due on April 15 of every year or the report is due on the boss's desk next Tuesday. These calendar times indicate a local organizational time. The April 15 tax deadline is timed within a cycle of financial record keeping and reporting based on financial events in the previous calendar year, but reported to us and the government early in the new year on forms familiar to taxpayers as W2, 1099, and so on. Tax review procedures occur afterward when we may be held accountable for the information we filed, but there are limited periods of liability and compulsory record keeping. So we can throw away most of our records after seven years. All of these temporalities bear on how we fill out our forms.

The report to the boss is in relation to the unfolding of a project, the internal temporality and deadlines of that project, expectations of the management, the promised customer delivery date, the quarterly corporate earnings report, and so on. All of these may bear to some degree on what we write to the boss on that Tuesday. Similarly, candidates' statements and political news are shaped by the closeness of the impending election, the unfolding electoral events, and the dynamics of forming new administrations after the elections. Events, sources available to journalists, and the interests of the readers all conspire to make the texts time-sensitive.

Even if we are not writing within a specific chronological frame for known events or known organizations, still our texts are likely used at certain moments within repetitive and predictable activity systems and action procedures. Parts manuals in auto garages are consulted at specific junctures such as in establishing inventory, costing and planning repairs, assembling correct parts for individual jobs, and in billing customers. The construction of such manuals (or their new electronic equivalents with even greater capabilities of integrating and facilitating functions) needs to be aware of these typical activities, to fit the moments of use. TV schedules similarly incorporate innovations to facilitate the scanning of alternatives during a free moment between shows or in planning out the evening's entertainment. So even though documents are created and consulted asynchronously and participants may be attending to documents through multisynchronous frames (either conflicting or coming together over a specific event), yet chronicity guides both writer and reader.

INFLUENCING THE FUTURE

Particular documents may have the generic or specific mandatory force in directing the production of a sequence of future documents. A city council announcement of a special election sets in motion a predictable sequence of print and speech genres. Likewise, a directive of a committee chair can set out a sequence of reports, reviews, and comments that will lead to a committee ballot on a proposal. This sequence may further set out an enforceable sequence of calendar dates for deadlines, filings, and actions.

Since all utterances are designed to have some influence or uptake they all speak not only to their moment but to the moments that follow. Some texts may embody specific designs for influence and aim at specific consequences: the home improvement loan application, the advertisement with a return form or discount coupon, the student essay that aims to have the teacher writing an A on top. Some documents may be embedded within institutions that carry out substantial consequences of the text—the judicial decree that can send someone to prison or set them free, the CEO's directive that can authorize a hefty bonus, the military order that will set assault teams in motion.

Sometimes that desired influence will be more modest: to gain the recognition that you have filed the necessary papers in a timely way so that you will not be penalized for negligence or to announce that you are aware of certain facts. The influence a text may seek on future events may be less clear-cut. Even a private journal of personal experiences affects the diarist's thinking, perceptions, and consequent actions. The diarist feels better or worse, more determined and focused on action or confused and uncertain, leading to inaction. The diarist comes up with phrases to be used in more public communications in the future, now that he or she knows his or her thoughts and feelings.

Because of this desire to influence future actions, the effectiveness of documents may be improved if we can reasonably project the moment at which the document will be taken up by others, under what conditions, constraints, and motives. For example, if we are writing a letter of application for a job, it may help us to be aware that the letter will go to a personnel officer reviewing documents for five different positions simultaneously, each of which may have a hundred applicants. And further, before the officer goes home today he or she must pick a short list of people to interview for each position. Those constraints may help us decide what would get favorable attention. What works under these conditions of reading and decision making, however, may not work when we are among a small hand-picked group invited to apply for an elite position, where our letter will be read and discussed carefully by a blue-ribbon committee and held in explicit comparison to the letters of three other hand-picked candidates. To have any hope of influencing future events in either case, we need some plausible sense of what those future moments would be like.

In those moments of uptake the readers usually only have a limited number of plausible actions to choose from. Being able to project this future can help shape our writing to better effect. If the applications are to be initially reviewed to select a short list for further interview, some issues may be premature to raise. On the other hand, if hiring happens directly from the application, we may want to be explicit about our requirements for pay and privileges.

Most wide-circulation publications as well have short shelf-lives, even if later they take on different existence as historical documents. Newspapers and online news sites measure life in hours and days. Magazine articles need to be of interest in the month of release, and any extended reprint life is a bonus. Most wide-circulation books need to gain popularity fast or vanish from the bookstore shelves within months; only a rare few books gain a long-standing place on publisher backlists. Even libraries, except for research libraries that need to keep an historical archive, periodically get rid of older books that no longer are of interest to the community. Research articles in scientific and scholarly journals may be read for a number of years, but only a few get noticed, read and cited as the years go on. Citation half-life, a concept from information sciences, measures the extinguishing relevance of research articles for current publications.

Writing that is intended for relevance to multiple readers over an extended period of time still has temporality. Self-help books are read by people at particular junctures in their lives; further, the tides of fashion, culture, and knowledge make likely that the book will eventually be dated. Textbooks are used with temporal sequences of classroom activities which the books must support; additionally, knowledge grows and changes—so a textbook usually must report the most current disciplinary findings while avoiding uncertain new results that may be discredited during the anticipated life of the book. Reference books, likewise, must walk the line between being current and being transiently faddish. The best way to assure a text some enduring life is for it to gain a central role in an enduring institution, such as a church, university, or a government not troubled by coups, revolutions, or reconstitutions. (I would mention the recent attempts of L. Ron Hubbard, Maharishi Mahesh Yogi, and Uzbekhi tyrants to live by this wisdom, but their attempts may evaporate soon, thereby dating this current book which I am trying to fit within the very slow rhythms of academic rhetorical theory, which even keeps alive fragments that predate Socrates). Of course, even if you get the work a safe institutional home, then the rhythms and patterns of institutional activity will still shape when and how the old book will be pulled out and read.

THE TIME WITHIN THE TEXT

Some texts are designed to fit within the rhythms of life—such as the phone book consulted when there is an immediate need for information. Any significant delay in finding the phone number, pulling the reader away from the pressures of life, will be a cause for irritation. Other texts, in contrast, are designed to remove us from the here and now—to help us forget a long airplane ride or to lift us from our living room easy chair to pre-Cambrian rain forests.

The texts used within daily time urgencies need to be designed for convenient and easy access during those activities and to provide desired resources for those other activities to justify whatever time out required for reference. The encyclopedia article must make its information easy to locate and must provide good and useful information worth the time to read paragraphs. During that period the reader enters encyclopedia time, becoming a processor of encyclopedic information, engaged in highly focused search for desired information and building up a schematic representation of the subject. But the reader also enters into a world of disrupted chronologies, of atomized parallel sequences that can be jumped across by cross-reference. The reader, familiar with the organization of such texts as encyclopedia articles or research papers, though, can restructure the order of reading and the amount of time devoted to various parts to meet personal need.

On the other hand most of our expectations and training of reading predispose readers to giving their time over to the writer. The writer then can sequence the movement through topics, holding various objects and ideas up for the reader's contemplation—lingering on some, passing rapidly through others, transforming ideas sequentially.

The writer may also attempt to control the temporal experience of the reader more minutely by controlling the rhythms of the text, the difficulties of the syntax, the technicality of the language, the digressions or explanations—or by the directness and simplicity of a narrative. The writer may try to make the reader stop and figure things out or hold up a multi-faceted object for wonder, or the writer may move the reader rapidly across a clearly marked landscape where pieces fall quickly in place.

While such issues may bring to mind the aesthetic concerns of poetry and fiction, they are pervasive in many kinds of daily texts. In an article in a management magazine the bulleted lists of advice facilitate the reader stopping to think about their own current situations and problems. An economics article in the same magazine may alternate between easy to read scenarios of business activities and short dense paragraphs of economic reasoning over which the reader may need to pause, but not too long, before being given another fast moving survey of the current economic landscape. Such issues are characteristically discussed under the heading of style—but they are as much a matter of moving the reader through states of consciousness, attention, and mood as they are about the specifics of the language used to do so.

In between these extremes of reader-timed texts and writer-timed texts are many middles. The writer may assist the reader in shuttling between alternative times and current concerns. The management article discussed just above are part of a class of self-help articles that do not so much tell the reader remarkably new things as give the reader a leisured opportunity to contemplate their current situation with the reminder of some familiar prescriptions. Other kinds of instructional and do-it-yourself texts provide guidance for a hands-on operation, but in a slowed-down instructional mode. A plumbing guide may take time to explain how valves work—for a moment transporting the reader inside the valve to notice the seating of the washers and the mechanisms of flow and interruption—so that the home-owner can diagnose and repair the leaky faucet.

Even the most abstracted intellectual texts may need to bring the reader out of the world of abstractions back down to their daily experience and concerns so they can understand concretely what the ideas mean in practice and perhaps identify moral or ethical applications. Spiritual books, for example, often mediate between the eternity of timeless truths inscribed in long-enduring sacred texts and the daily worries and puzzles of people taking time to contemplate their lives, relations, and souls.

Even fictions and entertainments draw on readers concerns, frustrations, and experiences of the daily world, pulling the readers from their street presence into an audience—as the old tradition of dramatic prologue explicitly did. Throughout the fiction daily experiences and life knowledge are transformed and played upon. Sometimes this worldly connection is explicit as in political satire or social problem literature, with perhaps some intention of transforming the audience's perception and experience of the world. Sometimes the connection with the world is more distant, as the audience is left only with a sense of refreshment, a reminder of emotions not felt in a while, and perhaps a different way of looking at people or events.

Texts have the potential of linking our time and other times overtly discussed in the text. An account of prior periods may exercise our historical imaginations, add to our knowledge, and draw us back to an earlier time for a few hours. It may also help us recognize our current moment as analogous or even continuous with earlier moments, so we see our contemporary concerns as part of larger flows of economic or political developments. Texts also introduce readers to alternative ways of thinking about time—as we perhaps first experience Proustian reminiscent time or we start to become aware of geologic time. Some texts give us means to think of ourselves positioned in that time—as accounts of biological and or cultural evolution may do. Texts further can make these time frames visible and important to us, helping us see the multiplicity of times in our lives. This transforming of our sense of our own time can change our ideational or ideological orientation to the embodied world. Chapter 10 of this volume will explore more fully how a writer can help direct and organize the reader's experience of time.

THE TEMPORALITY OF MULTIPLE TEXTS

Sequences of text, too, bring their temporality in how they represent our time and how they construct times for literate interchange. Emails may come rapidly on one another, pressing for immediate response, while journals have monthly or annual cycles and represent events with longer flows. Records of our life events, educations, and careers add up over a lifetime, while great intellectual and aesthetic traditions are seen in the flow of centuries.

Academic courses for the most part are linearly sequential processes, defined by the structured time of a syllabus. Major asynchronicities only arising from students' bending of deadlines and teachers' delays in returning marked papers—with well-known difficulties arising from both. The main potential source of multi-synchronicity is in the assigned readings that come from different times, places, and activity systems. Many classes avoid these complexities by only using a textbook of recent vintage that homogenizes and codifies knowledge in what appears to be a timeless way, but actually reflects an author-imposed consensus slightly behind the leading edge of disciplinary inquiry and controversy. Synchronic discontinuity is only foregrounded when textbooks are clearly out of date or late-breaking highly publicized findings directly contradict the book's teaching.

History and literature courses which consider temporally and culturally distant themes and materials, however, often introduce texts that are explicitly asynchronous with the classroom moment. That asynchronicity is foregrounded and managed by the standard classroom distinction of primary and secondary texts to be read in distinctively different ways—the primary to be interpreted as historical fact or privileged literary experience out of time, and the secondary as reliable knowledge in the synchronic now of the classroom. Only in more advanced classes in the subject, as students start reading multiple, conflicting texts are issues of multi-synchronous relations of texts usually dealt with. And even then, an official narrative of a main textbook may put all the developments into a normalized historical narrative, fitting all the texts within classroom time that unfolds from the handing out of the first day syllabus until completion of exam and posting of grades.

The task of attuning to asynchronous and multi-synchronous processes of literate interaction is more invisible and harder to monitor—but to people who have been engaged in an academic or professional specialty for a while, it is apparent who the newcomers are, those who may do things technically properly but don't know the underlying dynamics and pacing of the discussion and the most effective moments for intervention. Neophytes are characteristically judged as either too hesitant to enter when they need to or too quick to speech when they might wait for events to unfold a bit more.

Lawyers, for example, learn to juggle the asynchronicity and multi-synchronicity of relevant precedents, antiquated laws that have been reinterpreted in practice, larger judicial issues that are making their way up the court system, changing legislative mandates on county courts, the politics of impending district attorney elections, the particular events involving the victim and the accused, the commitments and habits of the presiding judge and the unfolding of this particular trial, with multiple filings, appeals, and actual courtroom events that lawyers must respond to. The complexity of events moving on different time scales is ignored at the client's peril.

TIME TO PRODUCE TEXTS

Finally, writers should consider the time it takes to develop a piece of writing—what has been called the writing process. During this process, a writer engages in many different kinds of activities that ultimately bear on the final text produced but that are not necessarily represented or manipulated in the final text. Early idea-generation activities differ from those that developed concrete plans, those that produced some text, and those directed at reviewing and improving produced text. Such differing activities are often identified by terms such as pre-writing, inventing, planning, draft-writing, revision, editing, and proofreading. People do not necessarily follow these activities in a simple-stage-like manner, but rather move around them in a recursive fashion. Further, people's processes turn out to be highly individualistic, depending on personal habits and tastes, along with the particular circumstances of each writing situation. Yet the overall sequence of activities helps a writer bring a text into being, emerging from first thoughts into polished prose.

Awareness that writing takes time and only gradually emerges through a variety of activities relieves a writer from the anxieties that come from a sense of incompletion and imperfection. Writers do not have to produce fully-formed text from the beginning. After all, writers are solving problems and figuring out what they have to say as they go along, so necessarily the partially emerged text will appear flawed and imperfect with problems still to be solved. Awareness of process opens up the temporal space of production as something to be thought about, worked with, perhaps rearranged or managed, rather than something to be simply painfully endured or to suppress from consciousness.

Even though writing processes may not always be carried out in a clearly marked stages with definitive borders as one moves from one stage to the next, the awareness that the writer's primary attention is now focused on one level of work, and that the writer can rely on one having previously thought through certain levels of work, and that other kinds of things will be worried about later, keeps the writer from having to feel compelled to juggle too many tasks at once. The writer can think about sketching out big ideas, or search for strong examples without having to worry about sentence coherence or spelling or accurate typing. All will be worried through and done in its time.

An awareness that processes vary according to personal habits, task, and situation, invites writers in each situation to articulate and improve their habits without imposing an uncomfortable general model. And it invites writers to think of the nature of the task and situation facing them and how their personal habits may be accommodated and exploited to advantage in any particular case. Chapter 12 of this volume provides further thoughts on the nature of writing processes and how they can be managed effectively.

The perspective on genre and activity systems presented in this book also provides additional dimensions to observing, understanding, and managing writing processes. Each genre suggests the kinds of resources that need to be drawn on and brought into it, the ways in which they should be typically represented, the aspects that will be evaluated and expected and therefore need to be attended to with special care, and thus the kind of work needed to produce those documents. If a psychological experiment will likely be evaluated on its methodologically correct and precise account of how the data was produced and recorded, a writer will design one's experiments and record the design and ensuing events so as to produce an accountable narrative of method. If an autobiographic reverie is dependent on the depth and richness of texture of memory, an essential part of the writing process is to find ways to tap into deep sensory memory. In writing for a job application, where judgments about competence are likely to be made on final appearance and formal correctness, then the writer might build in multiple end-of-the-process inspections.

Further, each genre just as it carries out typical forms and activities carries with it typical situations and processes of production, learned as part of learning the genre. Learning to write a news story occurs at the city hall, in making connections with informants, in conducting interviews, as well as at the keyboard. It involves learning how to keep a reporter's notebook and when to make an audio recording. It means learning when and where to compose a story so as to meet deadlines, but not too early to miss late-breaking events. It has to do with learning about the typical ways of the newsroom and the editor, and a thousand other things that old hands know about the profession in general and idiosyncratically at a particular newspaper.

The story of the newsroom highlights that processes of text production are embedded in the entire discursive activity system—and learning the genre and how to do it is learning the activity system, where the process of writing documents within the system fits in to all the ongoing activities, including editorial assignments, paper policies, and budget meetings. Further, it lets one know where the supports and resources are—the ongoing relationships with informants and public relations offices, the available files in the newspapers, the wire services.

One can even predispose audiences to positive reception of the text by engaging them in the production. Gaining the opinions of the upper management on what kind of information is needed in a business report and requesting access to relevant file, can increase the likelihood that the report will speak to their needs and perceptions in highly effective ways. Having the right people reviewing document drafts may turn these influential readers into committed advocates even before the document is released.

Every piece of writing is deeply embedded in some activity system, and the more deeply one understands that system and its rhythms, the more one can let the activity system help one produce the document—drawing on, being directed by, leaning against, and creatively resisting the ongoing welter of events, artifacts, resources, and personalities, to produce an emergent text that draws on the strengths of that system to be influential within it. Some students learn how to use the activity and rhythms of the class to build their papers and some never manage to get in the swing of things, so that they seem to be taking a correspondence course—sending in papers from cognitive, social, and temporal places that are distant from the activity of the classroom. A paper submitted three months after the end of the class, when the student and teacher are off doing and thinking about other things, goes without the supportive environment that surrounds other students writing to the same assignment. Strong writing draws on its time and speaks to its time. It knows when it is.

CHAPTER 4
THE WORLD OF TEXTS: INTERTEXTUALITY

The previous chapters have represented written texts (although they may appear to come from nowhere and to travel to everywhere) as always being contexted in the lives of the people who read and write and located in social spaces within which the texts circulate. The typification of genre draws participants together in recognizable activities and contexts crystallized by the genre. Even someone scratching an X on the ground where a hole is to be dug potentially evokes a history of maps (and even tales of pirate treasure)—or at least draws on a history of worksite inscription practices to identify specific places to be acted on.

Each new text can relate to prior texts in other ways. Sometimes the text may directly and self-consciously identify other texts it builds on or sets itself against; sometimes the reference is more implicit, but intentional; and sometimes the relation is entirely submerged, relying on familiar textual traditions and cultural resources.

Intertextuality is this relationship among texts, and it forms a separate domain or location within which texts can act. That is, intertextuality is both a resource activated in texts and forms a playing field upon which texts can assert their place, meaning, and consequence. The more deeply we understand the intertextual resources we inevitably draw on whenever we write, the more we will be able to manage, deploy, and position our writing with greatest clarity and intent upon this history of texts and how the readers may perceive those prior texts. And the more we understand how the texts we read also rely on prior texts, we can understand with greater clarity what they are trying to accomplish on which playing field, and whether we are satisfied with the kinds of intertextuality they construct.

INTERTEXTUALITY IS LIKE AND UNLIKE OTHER SPATIAL AND TEMPORAL NOTIONS OF CONTEXT

Texts are to some extent like interactions mediated in speech. A series of letters may serve in a friendship or a business relationship much as a series of turns in a conversation, so that each new utterance relies on and speaks to the previous ones and sequentially is part of the temporal unfolding of arrangements, relationships, and activities. But texts endure beyond our fading memories of previous conversations, and so we can look at them to refresh our memories, and we can refer to them as enduring artifacts in our new statements. We may even quote them. If memories of our readers differ, we can produce the prior letters, if we have saved them. Thus as texts add up into an archive they become a binding resource on the current moment, locating current events within a documentable space of prior texts.

Texts outside the immediate interchange may also come to be treated as relevant, becoming accountable facts within the interactional situation. We may introduce a prior contract that encumbers current negotiations. No matter what current participants in the negotiation wish, they must now recognize and respect the terms of the prior contract. Or, in another situation, we may refer to a shameful family secret revealed in a letter that Aunt Rosie sent us. Of course we could mention Aunt Rosie's spoken comments or could even suggest our respondent go speak to Aunt Rosie—but the enduringness and circulation of documents means that Aunt Rosie's divulging of that secret cannot be denied or radically misconstrued or misremembered. These circulating documents, both contract and personal secrets, may even be seen and read by numerous people not part of the original or the current communicative interaction unless we burn them or otherwise keep them hidden.

Networks of documents grow and circulate, and become mutually accessible, particularly after the inventions of print, cheap paper, and widespread literacy. Libraries, mass printings, and the transformative ease of digital communication and the World Wide Web means that there are extensive sets of documents that can be brought to bear on any new circumstance, written or spoken. Texts become accountable to wide bodies of prior texts which are deployable as resources.

The status of the intertext, nonetheless, remains tied to social and institutional arrangements that value texts and how texts become intertwined with social arrangements. Consider, for example, the history of the relation of oral and written contracts. Before writing, all agreements were oral. When writing entered the picture, writing was only used to remind people of spoken agreement. The written document only eventually gained the status of an enforceable contract as business law became a matter of record, and business records established accountability for business practices. Now spoken contracts have a much more dubious status and are harder to enforce, and all major agreements are reduced to writing, with the written form taking legal priority over any oral understandings (Tiersma, 2010).

With the coming of the Internet we now recognize a virtual world consisting of digital communications, representations, and interactions, yet this virtual world has been growing since the inception of literacy, as people started to orient toward collections of texts as significant parts of their worlds, to which they might appropriately respond with more texts. Texts bind together groups of people who have access to, interests in, or responsibilities toward particular kinds of documents. People in academic specialties are expected to be familiar with the literature of their fields so as to be able to contribute to that literature and apply it to cases where their expertise is called on. Lawyers need to keep up to date on the latest rulings as well as prior precedents and laws so as to have maximum resources in their own pleadings and to be able to counter the deployment of these texts by their opponents. Stamp collectors and aficionados of the fictions of Thomas Pynchon each have their bodies of texts that help form the substance and interactions of their socio-literate worlds. For millennia, pervasive intertextuality shaped the world of religious scholars devoted to sacred texts and commentaries; similarly, now pervasive intertextuality has come to remake the world of increasingly large numbers of people in economically advanced societies. Institutions of law, bureaucracy, government, corporations, finance, health care, science and social science, social welfare, academic research, entertainment, journalism, and publishing—to name just a few—transform our here and now lives in relation to deep archives of records, files, and knowledge. Through the work of intertextually-guided professionals, these archives become relevant for who we are, what we do, and how we are to be treated in the current moment. Over a century ago we recognized the formation of large white-collar workforce and more recently we have come to call ourselves the information society. The requirements for education and high levels of literacy have increased for those who wish to participate fully and establish high levels of agency in this new way of life. Everyone needs to be able to move through realms of texts as adeptly as they navigate the physical world, perhaps even more adeptly.

Bodies of texts not only provide a terrain against which new utterances may emerge, they have their own rhythms of temporality. Documents from the deep past may be rehabilitated and made immediately relevant, as when an ancient law or a philosophic argument is brought from the recesses of forgotten archives to be claimed to rule in a current case. Different domains have different relevancies for documents of different ages, and how prior texts may be recalled and made relevant to the moment at hand. Arguments may evolve slowly or rapidly based on whether significant, slowly maturing statements appear perhaps only several times in a century, or financial trades are transmitted and responded to in micro-seconds.

EXTENSIVENESS AND SHAPE OF INVOKED INTERTEXT

When we now write, our activity is likely to be already deeply embedded in one of the well-established activity systems relying on a robust intertextual infrastructure. This intertextual infrastructure contributes to defining the current moment as well as to the immediately relevant bodies of texts that need to be explicitly and implicitly considered in framing our response. A lawyer preparing contractual documents for a client must take into account the law and precedents for the nation and local jurisdiction that specifically regulate the kind of transaction being engaged. Even though none of the laws may be explicitly mentioned in the contract, the terms of the agreement must be in conformity with the provisions of the law, and lawyers would be well-advised to be mindful of the opportunities the laws provide for creating favorable terms for the client. Litigation precedents and rulings might also help guide the drafting of the document so as to be effective if it were to come to court. The contract also should be well positioned against the relevant business and financial documents that define the client's financial situation, obligations, plans, and wishes.

On the other hand, the lawyer need not attend to, nor in any way make the contract responsive, to many documents, both near and far from the matter at hand. In a real estate transaction, neither a newspaper description of the neighborhood the property is located in nor the history of the property itself is likely to be relevant to the effective contract—unless another lawyer does a great deal of work to establish the legal relevance to the case, perhaps to indicate the property has a different owner or contains toxic substances that are liable to legal regulation, thereby bringing it into the relevant intertext. Even less likely to bear on the case is the owner's childhood schoolwork or medical records. The lawyer needs to be careful in intertextually locating the contract in a complex textual world, but a fairly defined one. Although the law now rules life, it rules life primarily from the page, and anything that would come to notice to the law must wind up in the network of legally admissible documents that the law would consider relevant.

Although in a less compulsory way, philosophic arguments exist in a network of texts and anyone attempting to advance a new argument with any hope of credibility, even in an oral forum, must take into account a canon of prior authors that have puzzled over the question at hand. If the argument occurs among trained philosophers the expectation will be quite explicit, as the writer will be expected to take into account Aristotle's and Locke's positions, if the field has deemed that in fact Aristotle and Locke are the most relevant authors for the issue. Training in the field explicitly requires induction into the canon of texts deemed relevant and in the appropriate ways of framing issues, positioning one's views and arguing for new claims in the on-going discussions over the accumulated wisdom registered in the intertext. The training is equally in what texts and modes of argument are not germane. Even in non-expert, daily life discussion of philosophy, the more one is familiar with the kinds of objections and considerations posed in the history of philosophy, the better able one is to frame views and anticipate objections—as well as to solve problems that drive one to philosophize.

In an even less rigorously intertextually organized domain, every newspaper story is framed against the unfolding stories of the previous days, the longer flow of reported events likely to remain in the memories of the newspaper-reading public, and the stories of competing papers. Public documents and reports, academic research, or private papers may become relevant and referred to, or viewed as inappropriate or uninteresting to the news and therefore to be ignored—depending on readers' expectations and reporters' attempts to construct relevance. While neither law nor professional judgment may hold the newspapers accountable to awareness of the relevant intertext and the boundaries of the relevant, public memory, credibility, and interest will.

Every genre and activity system carries with it relevant intertexts to be drawn upon and to which they are held accountable. This may always be expanded by textual work that argues or insinuates the relevance of unanticipated documents, and parts of the anticipated intertext may be similarly excluded by authorial intent and strategy. Whole new intertextual systems may be made relevant, as when the affliction of a celebrity movie actor with a dread disease links health news with entertainment news for as long as the star holds the public attention and uses his or her celebrity to give attention to curing the disease. Also the magic of foregrounding and backgrounding as well as strategic remembering and forgetting, may change the apparent shape or immediate relevance of the intertext, varying according to the degree of inspection and compulsoriness of intertextual accountability.

It should be mentioned as well that each domain has its common practices of referring to and citing the intertext. Academic fields often foreground parts of the intertext through explicit citation following the differing conventions of various fields for footnotes or works cited, as specified in style guidebooks. Less explicit, though, is which parts of the intertext are left entirely in the background as "general knowledge" of the field, no longer attributed to any author. Also less explicit are the practices of representing material from the intertext, whether from extensive quotation and comment, paraphrase, summary, or just the passing use of a term originated by another author. Non-academic professional domains, such as law, accounting, and journalism, have their own regulations and practices of identifying the relevant intertexts through citation or explicit linking of documents. Some domains, at the other extreme, leave the intertext entirely implicit, as folk tales borrow freely from each other, remind us of other folk tales, and capture a world-view resonantly expressed across many texts.

THE INTERTEXT AS A VIRTUAL THEATER OF ACTION

Texts originally were fully integrated into daily non-textual activities, as cows and sheep were tallied in the meadow and barn and tax collectors carried their lists as they traveled the land. To some extent this is still true as the express delivery messenger carries an electronic device to one's doorstep, to be signed and inscribed at the moment of delivery of a package. But texts increasingly have retreated to the counting house, government office, academic library, the internet and other sites where texts can be readily collected, inspected, contemplated, and processed in the presence of other texts, apart from the realities represented, analyzed, or directed by the texts. Within such indoor worlds of reading and writing, calculation, contemplation, and design, the most immediate realities to be contemplated are those inscribed in other texts. Within the intertextual world, the world outside the page only becomes accessible and relevant when inscribed through the typical and accepted procedures of the activity system related to the intertextual field. Thus for the operations of physical and biological reality to enter into the discourse of science they must be observed, collected, and inscribed by acceptable procedures of experiment, observation, or other legitimized methods. Then they are usually further processed from the initial textual form as raw data into charts, tables, data bases and other textualized and textually processed aggregates. When we are talking about the environment and climate change, we are most immediately talking about data bases, climate models, equations, scientific papers, policy reports and other inscriptions produced, stored, consumed, and contemplated indoors. The warmth of a sunny day is only relevant insofar as it is recorded and brought indoors in a format that can be handled in the textual world. Chapter 9 of this volume provides more detailed treatment of how we can inscribe realities into our texts and link our texts to others to establish an intertextual domain of inscribed meanings.

In the inverse process, those documents that are most likely to be integrated with our material, experienced world—such as architectural drawings used to construct buildings or standards for automobile fuel consumption and exhaust— are likely to have spent much time indoors being produced and processed among other texts. Even the principles by which we conduct our personal relations are pervaded by the textual work of psychologists, sociologists, and health researchers that have led us to monitor and guide our behavior in new ways. The world of texts, and now what we call the virtual world of information, has thus changed the basic social and material landscape on which we live our lives.

CHAPTER 5

CHANGING THE LANDSCAPE: KAIROS, SOCIAL FACTS, AND SPEECH ACTS

Identifying a time and place of communication does not yet, in itself, provide a situation or motive for writing. A motive embodies a desire or need to change the situation—an felt exigency to remedy some shortcoming or imperfection, as well as a belief that language can somehow contribute to the desired change (according to Lloyd Bitzer's definition of rhetorical situation as an exigent situation marked by an imperfection that can be corrected by language (Bitzer, 1968). That is, the speaker or writer sees the need to get something done, the opportunity in the moment to do this and the means to accomplish this through language. At some moment we think "it is time to write a letter to get a mistaken charge off my account" or "I need finally to write that paper tonight in order to get credit for this course and gain my degree" or "This is the moment to offer a critical analysis of Balkan geopolitics."

CREATING AND INFLUENCING THE SITUATION IN THE HERE AND NOW

A situation only comes into consciousness and takes shape from a perception of exigency. An unseen and unperceived threat that kills before being noticed provokes no situation for action, exists outside consciousness and response. As we go through our daily life there are many things around us we do not notice or think about, let alone write about. We are not moved to do so, because we do not see them as relevant to our concerns and lives. It is only things we notice and interpret as consequential for us that prompt us to wonder whether they might be improved through our making of language.

While in our pleasant walk with friends across the field we may talk about the birds above or our shared memories of amusing events, but we probably would not be paying attention to the physical threat of runaway trucks until we see one careening toward us. We worry about writing papers for classes only when schools, courses, and degrees become significant in our lives. There are many people who currently have no thought of educational institutions, even though they may live around the corner from one; and there are enrolled students who have other things on their mind so that a looming paper deadline presents no exigency.

Conscious awareness and framing of a situation already has the seeds of a motive and action, elevating attention above the level of general monitoring of the environment. The sense of urgency turns the walk into a situation, turns the near automatic monthly payment of bills into a problem to be attended to, the professor's assigned essay into something that consumes our attention and energies. The perception of a situation then brings about the possibility of action and potential moments and means for action. While a perceived danger in which we see no site for resistance, action, or protection, leads us to watch our destruction helplessly, it is the hope of action that leads us to search for the opening and the means. If we perceive no means at hand to relieve a pervasive heat, no shade, no fan, no air-conditioned room, we cannot begin to frame an action, but if we believe that there may be an oasis beyond the horizon, we struggle to move, despite the effort and added threat. If we believe in the possibility of public resistance and democratic removal of an offending government, we look for opportunities to influence the public debate with an eye toward elections, which provide a social system for inscribing public wishes.

Despite the psychological nature of framing of a moment for action, if the rhetor is to be successful in accomplishing his or her ends, the perceptions are accountable to material and social conditions. Otherwise, one would risk being perceived as a foolish henny-penny warning that the sky is falling when listeners do not perceive the danger and cannot be made to see the danger. For them, there is no urgency to the situation and no imperfection, so the words are just untimely foolishness. If people feel no personal, physical or moral cost to a war, nor even perceive events as one of unusual hostility, it is difficult to have them oppose a war they do not notice or care about.

The rhetor has an easier task, of course, if the audience shares material and social experiences that predispose them to see the rhetor's framing of the moment as common sense, even more so if they share relevant sets of social typifications that would lead to congruent understandings of the immediate life world. If in response to a terrible attack witnessed by all and suffered by many, people anticipate that the government leader will speak and propose a call to action, they are ready to listen. The leader may then be able to call on them to engage in efforts that just the previous month would have been unthinkable.

While powerful rhetors may have some effect in reframing the situation and influencing people's judgments about events and appropriate actions, they can do so only by being attentive to the experience, perceptions, and available potentials of the situation. A situation may be transformed by the child announcing that the emperor has no clothes, but only if available observations or experiences can give credibility to the claim. As the story goes, the child blurts out his transformative truth while the naked king is parading in front of all to see.

CONDITIONS NOT OF OUR OWN MAKING, THAT WE CONSTANTLY REMAKE: SOCIAL FACTS AND SPEECH ACTS.

This role of social belief and experience, and the rhetor's perception of it, constitutes the symbolic side of Marx's (1937) famous comment that we make our lives but not in conditions of our own making. On the material side, a farmer may plow, fertilize, irrigate, and apply pesticides to fields, but that farmer must still be attentive to the initial conditions of soil, climate, and ecosystem, even though his or her actions may be able to transform them to some degree. Influencing humans through language is equally a matter of evaluating, selecting fields for action, and aligning to conditions even in the attempt to transform them. But instead of aligning to material conditions, what we must align with are social facts. Social facts are those things that because people believe are true, are therefore true in their consequences, in the formulation of W. I. Thomas (1923). Social facts are conditioned by and accountable to material conditions and the experiences available to people, but ultimately the symbolic world of communication must speak to the consciousnesses and emotional beings of our audiences. Our statements must become facts to them, part of the symbolic landscape they live in.

Acts of language create social facts that change the way people view their interior and exterior landscapes, the relations with those around them, their material conditions and themselves. This may be as simple, superficial, and emotionally neutral as presenting them an electric bill they will honor and write a check to pay. It can be as complex, profound, and wrenching as having them reconsider the decency and morality of people whose behavior contravenes their personal values. It can be accomplished in as familiar and formulaic a text as a utility bill, or it may take a complex innovative performance drawing on multiple traditions and hybrid textual forms that aggregate emotions and thoughts while disrupting and reorganizing expectations and frames of reference—as perhaps occur in powerful works of art. But each must became an unmistakable act that cannot be ignored or denied, and consequentially change the audience's mental landscape for action. They must become social facts by being successful speech acts.

The theory of speech acts can help us understand how this happens, and what we have to do to make this happen. Although developed only to characterize short verbal pronouncements (Austin, 1962; Searle, 1969) and presenting some difficulties in applying to extended written texts (see Bazerman, 1994), speech act theory presents the powerful insight that words do things, mediated through the alignment and understanding of others. Further, the theory notes that these acts then change the reality for future utterances through the perlocutionary uptake of the acts by listeners. But speech acts, the theory argues, accomplish these things only if crafted to meet conditions necessary for success, which Austin dubbed felicity conditions. These felicity conditions have to do in part with the external conditions under which an utterance was made: who has the rights to make the utterance, under what conditions and in what venue, with what timing and what attendant cooperation. A baby can be christened only by authorized clergy in a sanctified place and a law declared only by appropriate members of government carrying out the constituted procedures of the country through accepted institutional practices. Felicity conditions, however, also concern the manner and form in which the utterance is realized and with what understandings by both speaker and hearer. Thus in performing a wedding, the clergy or judge must meet some minimum ritual requirements of verbal performance, such as asking each of the participants whether they freely enter a union, to which there must be an affirmative response. But also the presiding official must also be of serious intent in carrying out this performance, as well as believed to be of serious intent by the participants. Similarly the serious intent of the married must be presumed in their acceptance; otherwise we would have a mock marriage, a fraud, a satire, or other act, but a failed marriage.

A further insight of speech act theory is that part of every speech act is a locutionary act—representing a certain state of affairs. In taking vows of marriage people either explicitly or implicitly represent that they are not already married to some other spouse. Again the act fails if the locutionary representation turns out not to be true—or more precisely taken to be true by the relevant parties. The speech act can fail and the marriage be declared invalid if a prior and still valid spouse appears. But if the act is accepted as true, the representations or implied representations are taken to be true. Thus speech acts create both the facts of the accomplished action plus acquiescence to the explicit or implied representations that are asserted as part of the act.

This concept of speech act then provides the mechanism by which our words can influence the world and remedy imperfections in situations. Speech acts change the social world by creating new social facts, which change what we believe, how we interact socially, and how we act in the world. These social facts then may even change our relation to the material world. If we believe the world is flat, with edges one can fall off of, we may lose enthusiasm for long sea journeys to unknown parts, while a conviction of the earth's roundness extends our adventurousness and knowledge. If common social beliefs hold that there is little you can do about the weather, that a certain number of climate disasters are inevitable and to be expected, and that free markets always respond creatively and successfully to changing conditions, then it is hard to mobilize changes in energy and pollution policy to combat global warming. On the other hand, if scientific argument convinces the public and policy-makers that global warming is occurring and will have catastrophic consequences too large to be absorbed by typical social processes, and further that certain of our actions can ameliorate the situation, then we will look at and act with respect to our environment differently. Of course, changing material experiences (such as rises in aggregate global temperatures, increases in violent weather, rising sea levels, and desertification) may also attune people to attend to different realms of social facts, thereby changing their beliefs and orientations to action.

Let us consider a more ordinary and less extreme example of how this nexus of rhetorical situation, speech act, social fact, and genre can work together to make possible effective action. Consider a person contemplating a lack of opportunities in the local job market and the sterility of his or her current occupation (in an attempt to create his or her own life, but not in a situation of his or her own making or even liking). Clearly the person sees an imperfection in the situation, but how could it be corrected, how could life be made a little more perfect? Noting that in the local economy people with university degree have more opportunities, the unhappy employee might desire to obtain a degree. Of course the person could just add a line to their resume, but that speech act is likely to fail in creating a robust social fact, as any potential employer has the intertextual resource of university records against which to hold the educational claim accountable. In such a case the social fact likely to be created is not the status of a university graduate but of a liar. Other short cuts such as paying a few hundred dollars to a diploma mill to create a record are again likely not to garner the full respect and credentials needed.

So there seems no path but to spend some time in an accredited institution which will entail many documentary speech acts, such as exams, papers, registration forms, and bill payments. Now, let us look in detail at one of the earliest series of written actions that must be carried out to set this in motion. Once having settled on an appropriate school to attend, to gain the status of student, the person must first apply, which means not only locating the application materials from the complex set of intertexts that constitute the university recruitment and application systems, but then filling them out. To complete the application materials the would-be student must write a variety of representations of information in the proper form, asserting many facts about identity, experience, prior educational accomplishment, and similar topics. The would-be student may also need to write an extended statement, take some exams, and fill out forms to have the scores forwarded from the exam agency. The would-be student must also solicit letters of recommendation and transcripts from previous schools. If the would-be student manages to felicitously collect all these documents and appropriately inscribe them within the university application system, he or she would then have completed the successful speech act of making application, and may receive a written (perhaps electronic) acknowledgment of this fact. The university cannot now deny that the person has applied. The applicant has met all the felicity conditions and a social fact has been created. Of course, if later it is found out that some documents were forged or falsified, the application can be declared invalid and the social fact erased. That possibility aside, that accomplishment is, however, hardly the end of the story, because the person now having achieved the status of applicant desires to be an accepted applicant. This requires that the application meet other felicity conditions arising from the evaluation of the elements inscribed in the application. The admissions evaluators may consider how well the prior academic record, entry exam scores, and quality of the letters and essays match the university's mission, and expectations of the university and compare to the records of other applicants. Even though these considerations involve evaluation by the reader, we can equally say the applicant wishes to meet them felicitously. The obsession of the college-bound is of course to anticipate and meet these somewhat fuzzier felicity conditions, so that the evaluators and they will be made happy. If the applicant is able to meet all these conditions in the application, the evaluators will inscribe another document granting the applicant the status of an accepted student. This then is just the beginning of further sets of inscriptions that accomplish becoming a registered and enrolled student in good standing, and then completing a record over the ensuing years that would establish the social fact and status of being a college graduate. Each of these steps could be analyzed in terms of what must be accomplished against more or less well articulated felicity conditions, that may be rule-governed or more dependent on the judgment of those who read and act on student inscriptions, for example grading student assignments.

From the institutional side, of course, the university would be somewhat imperfect if it lacked students, so it itself must create documents and procedures that would recruit and induce students into the university, accomplishing the enrollment of a select body of people transformed into matriculated students. Similarly the university must go about recruiting and maintaining a faculty, taking a thousand actions and building many systems that constitute the entire system of the university. Thus the social facts of universities and educated students are accomplished through the means of documents by which the system is organized, activated, and realized—accompanied by all the attendant face-to-face and material actions that are implied and give credibility to the documents, making the degree a meaningful one, by whatever standards of meaningfulness the various participants and surrounding society may invoke.

KAIROS AND EXIGENCY IN EMBODIED FACE-TO-FACE SITUATIONS

The face-to-face situation of spoken language, the physical environment and the visible social relations of co-participants often can lend a concreteness to rhetorical moments that help align participants to common understandings of what is going on and what is needed. The forest is burning around us, and the apparent urgency of the situation will help others understand your cry for help and will lend credibility to your claims and the exigency. Further if you are yelling down from a high point and looking off into the distance, your relationship to your hearers and the physical surroundings will be further defined and again your comments made easier to understand, to be aligned toward, to be credible, and to be influenced by.

Observable social and material conditions can aid the ready production of shared social facts upon which all will act. Team sports players can make their words intelligible to teammates even under the most difficult auditory conditions because there is so much visible co-orientation on the court or field and because of long common training that makes responses habitually anticipatable. Two friends watching a movie together can make comments cryptic to others, but hilarious to each other in the moment. As we say when asked what went on, "You had to be there."

In such real-time, physically embodied rhetorical moments the language helps focus and organize our orientation to the situation. The speech acts are readily interpretable as part of the events. Further, they are immediately and materially effective within the here and now, and participants can often observe the rapidly evolving consequences which mark the effectivity and social meaning of the acts. People start spraying fire retardant, someone passes you the ball, or your friends laugh—or they don't.

Some written communications can also be highly embedded in circumstances—fire teams can send out text alerts, sports coaches can chalkboard messages from the sidelines, friends in a silent auditorium could be texting each other. Typically the conditions of writing, however, are more removed from the immediate surroundings, with the writer and reader not visible to each other and separated by time. Nonetheless, it may be that on each end of the transaction each is engaged in material real-time activities that are coordinated by the text. The cookbook writer likely starts in the kitchen (no matter how desk-bound the composing and production process might become) and the reader may refer to the grease-stained cookbook open on the countertop while following the recipe. The invoice informs the shipping clerk which items to put in the cartons, the receiving clerk what to confirm, and the bookkeeper how large a check to write. The reporter interviews the political candidate and attends political events to create stories to provide citizens information that may affect how they vote.

KAIROS AND EXIGENCY IN THE INTERTEXT

In these examples, however, the scene of action becomes increasingly mental and cognitive. As discussed in the previous chapter, literacy has facilitated the development of a virtual world of the intertext, and that intertext itself can become the scene of action—the place where the rhetor can perceive an exigency and an imperfection. Voters need information that they get in the newspapers. A candidate has not gone on the record on the issue of school privatization and the reporter perceives the public might be interested in knowing the candidates' views. By interview and other means the writer gathers information for a story to appear in the newspaper, thereby establishing the candidate's position (that is, if the story meets the felicity conditions of a credible news story and is not effectively contested and thereby made dubious as a speech act and social fact). If we remove the temporal and geographical focus of an election, and the special relevancy status of voting citizen in the jurisdiction, we go one step further into the virtual world. The threat of global warming and the ongoing international negotiations on environmental policy may provide some material and social exigency to work in climate science, but more typically work in climate science, as in the other sciences, appears as a more generalized contribution to the scientific literature moving at its own pace. While scientists may know each other, the work is presented as though it were to anyone knowledgeable and committed in the field. The only exigency is that there is something we don't know yet and the scientist through the work offers an increment of knowledge. The imperfection is in the literature which has not yet fully examined some aspect of knowledge (as is highlighted in Swales' model of the scientific article introduction, 1990). The language remedy is the felicitous report of a credible scientific study. Similarly the exigency of a literary critic may appear even more out of time and space— that we do not understand a poem or playwright as deeply as we might, or we have been lacking some knowledge about a novelist's relationship with their publisher that would shed further light on her famous works. The imperfection in knowledge and interpretive depth is resolved by a work of scholarship. The scene of action is perceived in the text and the text's relation to other texts, only available through interpretation of the inscribed words.

The formation of kairos within the intertextual world has been a gradual historical phenomenon, accelerating in the last few centuries as robust intertextual systems have emerged whose relation to here and now experience is highly mediated through texts. To deal with a land dispute effectively these days, you do not now go out and put up a fence or stand your ground with a weapon. You enter into a complex intertextual world of deeds, registry, real estate law, filings—and maybe a surveyor to inscribe your land according to the directives of documents. To measure your wealth you no longer open your treasure chest to bathe your hands in jewels, but you go into your office to gather documents or examine a spreadsheet. Even to know if you feel healthy, while you still might give some credence to your gut feeling, you need to consult your medical records and results of tests. And to seek wisdom, while you still might seek a personal guru, you are likely to read a few books that define the tradition the guru is embedded in.

The intertextual world presents special difficulties for identifying rhetorical moments, the right times for utterance, in that we are less likely to have events unfolding in front of our eyes to excite, move or frighten us into writing—as the fire racing toward us will induce us to yell help. Similarly we have fewer immediate means to align our readers to an urgent here and now in which they must attend to our texts—let alone in the spirit and orientation and roles we would hope. It is one of the tricks of robust intertextual systems in fact to create exigencies for us to attend to texts, often through some institutional structuring that creates penalties or rewards, framed by deadlines. If we wish to maintain health benefits, we must fill out a form by a certain date and supply specific information. With web forms we cannot even file the document unless all required fields are filled in appropriately—before the page times out. And sometimes the information we provide is immediately checked out against other databases for consistency and accuracy. Further, unless we provide acceptable information we may not be able to proceed to the next page where the information we desire is located. While such devices are so effective we may not even think about them, these urgencies are rhetorical accomplishments. These exigency devices are worth understanding so we can know our options for responsive action better, and so we can mobilize them for our own purposes to assemble virtual kairos.

Understanding kairos within intertextual domains first requires an understanding of why the intertext matters to us. Given modern conditions of life, for example, institutional records about us (payroll, school, police, credit, health) might affect whether we are hired on a job, get a loan, get insurance coverage or get appropriate medical treatment. Further, we understand typically how a flaw in those records affects us—getting less pay than we are owed, having a mark on the record that would stigmatize us, or not having the records that would grant us preferred status. If we consider these imperfections of the record serious enough to be worth the effort and if we see means to modify or re-inscribe the record, we might then accept the exigency and attempt to have our payroll deductions adjusted, or have a juvenile arrest expunged from our record, or go through the effort of taking additional courses to complete the requirements for a degree. Given the use cycles of institutional records we can often anticipate when they are likely to be used and when might be the best time to modify them. Shortly before we wish to apply for a loan we may feel moved to check our credit rating so we can boost it if necessary. Educational records may become most significant at times of employment or application to further education, but the best time to remedy them is while we are still students. On the other hand, we may have no successful means with an acceptable cost of time, effort, money, or social displacement (such as by going underground and creating a new identity) to change the records.

In each of these cases, we also need to be aware of the effective means of changing the record that forms the intertext for our further actions—that is, what felicity conditions must be met and how. We must determine how we can demonstrate to the payroll office that we were due a raise, how we can prove to the credit bureau there is an inaccuracy, how we can build an academic record. This involves such things as establishing the credibility and authority to act in the circumstances, acting at proper times in proper ways, with proper verifiable supporting materials, doing whatever work is implied in the desired inscription, adopting the appropriate stances and relationships to institutions, and submitting the request in proper form in a timely way with all the relevant information.

We can either attend to the institutional facts residing in our records to protect our interests or we let them slide and live with the consequences, but they are undeniably parts of lives. Our stake in other intertexts may be more matters of our recognition and active pursuit of them. We may not care much about municipal noise pollution regulations until our neighbor adopts a pack of highly excitable hunting hounds. Even then we need to become aware that such regulations exist and are invocable, and then we need to learn the procedures for filing a complaint and presenting evidence. Even then we must decide whether invoking these procedures is worth the social costs of turning a neighborly relationship into a municipal documentary one, with all the consequent legality that might ensue. Similarly, we calibrate our attention to the news, how much of what sort we attend to, and which we act upon. Do we follow the news to consider the business consequences and modify our portfolio, or to ponder how we will inscribe our votes, or to hold our own in casual conversations? Are we political comedians who must every day write new jokes about current events to earn our living? At what point and why do we feel the need to enter into a blog discussion or write a letter to the editor, or begin to compose our own satires? Where is the stake, what is the imperfection, what are the effective means at hand, what is the timing, who is the audience? And then how can we draw the readers into the same sense of exigency and situation we perceive so that they will find our comments germane and worth attending to, our humor funny?

Such questions add new dimensions to the strategics of rhetoric, which was initially conceived in a world of face-to-face interactions, where social facts took shape in the here and now of mutual alignment in the moment. Indeed many professions, careers and life projects are now devoted to building, maintaining, and transforming the intertext in recognition of its importance for modern lives. The most visible professions have been those who physically produce and maintain the texts that provide the intellectual infrastructure—printers, publishers, librarians, writers. These intertextual workers now include those who build the electronic infrastructure within which information technologies reside, and those who inscribe meaning in digital spaces. This in effect can mean anyone who spends much of the day at the computer or working with documents, from bureaucratic clerks to lawyers to market traders to academics—each of them has the problem of aligning to a communal intertext and refiguring that intertext to incorporate or take account of their work, to create new social facts that will be visible and consequential for those that attend to that textual informational space. Meeting the well-articulated mandatory felicity conditions as well as the more suasive, strategic conditions that invoke readers' selective attention, evaluation, and memory form the basis of successful action.

CHAPTER 6

EMERGENT MOTIVES, SITUATIONS, FORMS

Writing requires extended work over time to create a verbal artifact that can work its effect, often at some physical (temporal and geographic) distance from the site of its creation. Such extended work directed toward distant ends requires we become aware of and understand our motives, so that we attend to them despite distractions and obstacles in our immediate environment. Good writing is aided by locating and nurturing our motivations.

Our motivations in any writing situation occur at the intersection of our long-term concerns and the emergent situation, recognized and given shape by our typifications about how situations are organized and the forms of action available in such situations. That is, our genre and situation shaped perceptions of openings for immediate action serve to crystallize underlying concerns and interests that lie behind our sense of imperfection in that situation.

Sometimes the motive is obvious to us, as familiar and compelling circumstances call on us to adopt a role and take a well-defined action. For example, when we arrive for a medical appointment we are given a form to fill out reporting our medical history. We are already in the role of seeking medical help, and we understand that the medical providers need information from us so that they can do their task well. We know we do not want to wait long for our appointment and we set directly to filling out forms so as not to fall back in the queue waiting for attention. Pressing circumstances cast us into a role. Often, though, our more ambitious and difficult writing tasks occur separated from the circumstances we are responding to and we must write without the immediate pressure of events unfolding around us at the moment. In such cases our motives may only take shape as we start to contemplate and give mental definition to our situation and then begin to plan and carry out actions. In this process the possibilities of action begin to unfold which in turn crystallize our motives for concrete objectives.

TYPIFIED MOTIVES AND FORMS OF ACTION

On one extreme our motive for writing may come from the need for social or legal compliance. Mandatory writing tasks often come to us in regulated forms on regulated occasions. We then either participate or visibly resist with consequence. If we participate, our influence is only in inscribing our compliance within the regulated forms of participation, within the allowable ranges of freedom. A clerk or other bureaucratic subordinate filling in forms at a computer terminal has only limited influence in what he or she inscribes as detailed information within the form, though there are some decisions to be made about the exact information and the form it is to be presented that might benefit or penalize the client. Electronic systems have increased the use of forms and held them more tightly to narrow standards, to the point of immediately rejecting a response if it does not contain all required elements in the expected form. Electronic systems may even check the accuracy of information by matching it with related forms and databases, so that credit card numbers must match with accounts, and case records must match with already existing case files before the response is accepted and we are allowed to continue. Yet still we do have some choices about the information we include to represent ourselves and our interests—whether which phone number we inscribe or what we list as a cause for complaint and how we elaborate in an available open field.

At the other extreme are self-chosen genres in situations of personal choice. No one except the philosopher him or herself determines what topic and discussion to address at what moment in time, and in which of the professionally acceptable genres. Poets may write when the spirit moves them and in the form that their impulses dictate. Political bloggers can take up topics and develop them when and how they see fit, within the flexible space with generic variety that blogs allow. Little other than personal impulse compels an individual in most cases to take on the role and voice of a poet or a philosopher or political blogger.

Many intermediate cases combine a degree of social compulsion with individual choice making about topic, substance, and genre, as well as the underlying motives that might be served. Assigned work in academic settings often provides substantial room for students to pursue curiosities, resolve personal puzzles, or assert identities and commitments. Journalists or their editors have degrees of freedom to select which stories to develop and columnists to decide on topics, stances, and approaches.

Even when confronted with social compulsion our motives are important to determine whether we will comply rapidly and willingly, whether we will be evasive and minimally compliant, or even deceptive and subversive. Depending on the nature and personal importance of our motives we can decide not to comply with the request, or even to actively resist the requirement. In cases where there are more readily available degrees of freedom our motives can play a much more integral role in how we respond, and thus the kinds of texts we will produce. Sometimes our feelings about the role we are cast into are complex and mixed; consequently, even though we may consciously believe we are committed to a writing task we act reluctantly. Chapter 12 considers psychological ambivalences, whether real or chimerical, we may have toward writing, so that we can overcome them to write with our whole heart and energy.

EMERGENT MOTIVATIONS IN EMERGENT SITES OF ACTION

Emergent motivations take shape when felt discomfort begins to meet locatable sites for action. The force for action grows as the site takes shape. We may even see an imperfection that we can name and would like to remedy, but until we locate a possible site for remedying it is an unscratched itch. For example, a student's interest in how local governments work may have been whetted by a summer internship in the local parks department which left her wondering about certain seemingly irrational policies. This curiosity then supports a decision to register for a political science course on municipal government. As she is introduced to different theories and examples her experience becomes a touchpoint for thinking about what she is learning. When assigned to write a paper about planning processes, she takes the assignment as an opportunity to look into parks planning and how the policies that troubled her came about. In the course of doing research she then uncovers a long-standing set of conflicts among homeowners, renters, businesses, and real estate interests, which becomes the topic of the paper. As she gets into the project, she realizes she may be deviating from the assigned paper. She then visits the professor to see whether she can renegotiate the assignment.

On the other hand the irrationality of her experience in the parks department could have taken her in very different directions if she started seeing herself as an advocate for people who were hurt by the policies, or if she were taking a creative writing major and were looking for material for a short story, or if she worked at a comedy club and were looking for material about the absurdities of daily work life.

Of course, which way we go to scratch an itch is a mixture of estimates of what else in our life we know about and are doing, how we perceive our established and emergent identities, what kinds of support are around us, and estimates of our ability to successfully carry out work in the corresponding genres. In thinking about the consequences of our actions we may also consider the likelihood of gathering an audience who will understand and be engaged in our meanings created in the genre we work in. Thus our motivations emerge and take shape in a complex world.

Effective writing is aided when we understand a wider repertoire of possible directions and have a wider range of skills to form our emergent motivations into a greater range of potential objects—so that we don't always follow the most obvious, well-worn and least demanding path—though often that may in fact be the best solution. If we want to buy a product, filling in the online order form according to exact instructions, as we have done many times before, will most efficiently meet our needs, even if it is not particularly challenging. We may even be bored by it, especially if we have to fill out twenty forms for twenty different products.

To pursue a bit more complex example, our desire to get to work, get around town, and visit our friends may be facilitated by having a driver's license. Obtaining a license requires filling out forms, passing tests, and registering at the Department of Motor Vehicles. The motives to enter the documentary system of the department of motor vehicles are extremely powerful—as anyone who has observed an adolescent in the United States or other developed country knows only too well. It is easy to follow that path, hard to avoid it, and writing the forms and taking the tests is not all that demanding. It is the obvious solution. Nonetheless, costs of car ownership and insurance, likelihood of traffic congestions, and looming global warming may in the long run may make one think about alternative forms of action and may even lead one to become a motivated environmental activist. These solutions, however, will take much more time and work, and require one to write far more effectively in far more difficult circumstances to much wider, conflicting audiences than filling out a few forms for a clerk whose task it is to facilitate and accept properly filled out forms.

On the other hand, understanding the alternative paths our motives may take us into more fundamental workings of society, can open the doors to greater influence on how we live, provide us deeper forms of engagement, and challenge us to more effective writing to more significant ends. Yet, even though such a path may lead us to take less expected actions and require from us more creative, less anticipated writing for which we must solve many novel problems, we cannot leave typification behind. Typification rules in originality as well as in the most boring and conventionalized task. The further we contest the taken-for-granted, the further we wander from the absolutely conventional, the more we must understand and use typification. For example, the environmental activist might need to deal with genres from science and engineering, governmental regulation and planning, public advocacy and organization, journalism and opinion, litigation, fund raising and NGO administration, as well as the specialized genres of environmental impact assessment and environmental modeling. Further, the environmentalist may need to take standard genres and invest them with new motives and forces, as when a class action suit is filed in a case arguing not about financial damage (typical for such suits), but an inequitable burden of environmental degradation on one community.

These complexes of genres, hybridization, and multiple choices only come into our view over time. The more we engage in a project and we map the situation and our opportunities, the clearer it becomes to us what we can and want to do. Thus it is inevitable that much of our learning to write occurs "on the job" (or in the community), insofar as we recognize that writing is part of the job and we invest time and energy into advancing our skill to carry out the job. As we get drawn into the motives and opportunities of our sites of engagement, we see how we can go beyond the most typified forms of action that were immediately apparent. This learning coincides with us taking on new identities, presences, and power within these socially organized activities.

While engagement with each new field of action brings learning about the literate opportunities of that field, we bring the experiences, tools, and skills of our prior writing engagements—as we move from one organization to another, as we move from one area of public action to another, as we move from advertising to public relations, as we move from journalism to non-fiction writing. In each case the prior experiences with literacy give us confidence and analytical abilities to frame writing problems and a range of tools and models to draw on. At times the tasks are similar and we can diagnose key issues quickly so we can readjust to modified circumstances, though creative action may still require deeper local analysis. But often the cultures and practices of the new domain of action are substantially different, so we must learn a new way of doing things even before we try anything unusual. When our area of endeavor switches entirely, such as when moving from marketing electronics to organizing famine relief, we must address new values, purposes, systems, relations, and cultures; and we must adopt new stances, genres, and styles to accomplish very different kinds of work. In the course of this the motives attached to writing change—and thus the very nature of the act.

SCHOOL WRITING, SCHOOL SITUATION, AND SCHOOL MOTIVES

The biggest leap most people make in their writing is from schooling to whatever they write outside of school. By that time people have spent so many years in schooling, and so much of their experience in writing has been carried out in school, it is often hard for them to see writing in any other than school terms. The school experience of writing becomes a general characterization of all writing, and the values and practices of school writing get carried over to non-school situations in ways that are inappropriate. While school provides many tools and facilities that can be of value, unless the transfer is intelligent and thoughtful, the practices of school can be limiting or even misleading. Thus people who do learn to use writing successfully in the world often say they only learned to write once they have left school. Many others say they never really wrote once they left school, or they write only privately. They never have made a real leap from the writing they learned to do in school to the tasks and opportunities the world presents them with. Insofar as they engage with new opportunities, they may discount them as real writing, thereby limiting their ability to think about these new writing situations creatively and to reflectively transfer and reconfigure what they have learned in school for new purposes.

Therefore it is worth spending some time to sort out the relationship between writing in school and writing elsewhere, so we can understand the transition and manage it more effectively. Such thinking can also guide teaching to better to prepare people for the transition. One of the characteristics of learning to write in school is that it is a time apart from the ordinary activities of life in order to enhance our life—through learning skills like the three R's, or engaging in the arts, or contemplating our values, or acquiring specialized forms of knowledge and practice, such as associated with engineering. When we finish schooling we are expected to take on various roles in the world, but while in school our primary engagement is with schooling itself. We learn about how to do school assignments; how to advance and gain rewards in schooling; how to use to advantage the minor institutional genres around the edges—whether excuse and doctor's notes, hall passes, or petitions for exceptions to regulations; and how to participate in the culture of students through note passing, secret peer notebooks, or sponsored activities like newspapers.

The central writing activities in school are framed as assignments set by the curriculum and instructors in fulfillment of the courses, and they are evaluated by the instructors or outside evaluators to see whether we can demonstrate the required knowledge and competence. That is, our writing is evaluated and corrected in relation to the curriculum. Our motives typically are minimally to get school done and maximally to get school done well. Both are usually associated with a grade and avoiding correction—and sometimes with praise for exceptional achievement. Consequentially, some of the most important writing is associated with examinations—local, state, and national. These examinations may then define the taught curriculum which shapes the tasks, attitudes, and skills associated with more daily writing. This basic institutional structure can be supplemented by values of interaction and engagement—the teacher caring about what you are writing and responding to the thoughts you express, whether about your personal life or subject matters like history in order to mentor you to more sophisticated thought. Yet the personal response is still that of a teacher and not a parent or friend, and even the most engaged dialogue on subject matter, whether of mentor/mentee, or erstwhile colleague to established scholar, is within the frame of academic subject matters within an educational environment—where the primary work is the development of individuals. The student writer is the object of development—whether being regularly evaluated and corrected, or supported, encouraged, and led into rewarding halls of learning. Only when the upper ends of education intersect with actual professions, disciplines, arts, or service activities do educational practices begin to overlap robustly with practices in the world. And even then students always know that the educational reality of teacher assessment based on student display of skills and knowledge makes the school writing different from business where the final test is a profit or a building that does not collapse (Becker, Geer & Hughes, 1968; Dias, Pare, Freedman, & Medway, 1999).

In addition to evaluation with attendant punishments and rewards, several other aspects of schooling limit our ability to engage more deeply in other forms of writing. The practice of teachers setting assignments is essential to challenging the students and keeping them on the learning task; the practice, however, limits students' ability to identify meaningful writing situations which they may want to respond to and thus does not nurture their ability to identify motives to write outside assignments. Writing is thus not seen as an actively invoked tool for personally felt tasks in personally perceived situations. Rather writing is something assigned by others, with the writer searching for a successful way to fulfill the assignment—at best the student can locate a topic or approach he or she is interested in and cares about within the frame of the assignment. Further, writing assignments often are made only to practice writing skills rather than pursuing a substantive interest in the content or action. When a substantive task is assigned, it is frequently a faux action, such as pretending to write a letter of complaint about a product, but not sending it because it is not part of a real situation and need. Further when presumably writing about substantive maters in their various subject courses, students are rarely asked questions that the instructor/examiner doesn't already know the answers to, so even then the writing is about display of knowledge and analytic skills rather than sharing of valued thoughts and information. Finally, assignments are often part of a very short sequence of interactions, so that the student writer is always in the position of starting up a fresh conversation, even initiating it—with all the uncertainties about the audience, the topic, the issue at hand that usually attends first meetings. The student writer rarely gets the sense of being in a long conversation with extensive back and forth—focusing and strengthening motives, forming a relationship with the interlocutor, and developing issues and content at play in the conversation. Rather the writer is always in the position of warming up, trying to get something going.

As a consequence of these characteristics of school writing, for most people writing is about pursuing correctness, being evaluated, and displaying knowledge and skills. The motives most deeply attached to writing are avoiding embarrassment and gaining approval. No matter how deftly the evaluations are given, students' imaginations of what can be accomplished in writing are limited, and their motivations are often heavily freighted by aversive emotions and fear of being found wanting. The student is not prepared to see writing simply as performing a task successfully, so that it meets the conditions to do what it has to do. Anything of this character in the school context is not counted as writing—just filling out a form—and therefore is not a serious exercise of skill. Even when tasks engage other situations and motives, they are still infused with school situations and dynamics.

School-based standards of writing seem to endure long past the context of school, rather than standards drawn from the tasks of the world. I regularly hear from lawyers or scientists that those who write best are those who use poetic figures, wide vocabularies, and other marks of school approved writing rather than getting the job done—whether explaining the theory and evidence clearly or making a persuasive case for a client. While training in school can provide basic tools, habits, and practice, the situation and motives of school are distinct from those of other activities. Not understanding the differences of school writing and writing elsewhere can be an obstacle to addressing new tasks successfully and may even prevent people from taking on new challenges, as they feel the weight of school experiences too heavy to confront. Consequently, they never develop a long term engagement in a field of writing that is personally meaningful and they never develop motives and commitments that will keep them working at the hard task of writing that will lead to high levels of accomplishment.

GRADUAL EVOLUTION OF SITUATION
AND OUR MOTIVES WITHIN IT

Just as we spend many years learning how to be students, it takes a while to learn the landscape of new domains, become familiar with the genres and the associated activities and dynamics, identify our opportunities to intervene by writing, and the repertoire of devices, styles, phrases, and tactics that are effective in the relevant genres. As we develop these skills we may also develop a higher level of understanding of how the entire system we are participating in works, so we can become more strategic about when and why we write. As we learn these things, we also re-form ourselves, taking on identities, stances, and commitments that give focus and strength to what we do as writers, how we project ourselves as writers, and what we attempt to accomplish through our writing. We move past the awkwardness and uncertainty of beginnings in unfamiliar social situations, to knowing the people we are communicating with, what we want to communicate, what will work, and where next we may take the conversation. We learn this by continually writing within a world where we see the effect or lack of effect of what we do.

Even within a single episode of writing there can be a substantial evolution, as the writing process occurs over time and each step we take in the writing gives more focus and shape to the situation. We get a more refined and directed idea of where we are going with each step we take. We can look on what we have produced so far and reflect on what is coming into being and refine it, as the later chapters of this volume will explore.

An even more significant evolution can occur as an interaction develops over time, so that problems get defined, roles of participants emerge, work to be accomplished becomes clearer, facts of the situation and relevant knowledge become salient—in short we know a lot more of what we are doing in a place we have become more familiar with. Sometimes our motives may in fact change as we come to see what is possible and impossible, or we come to recognize new opportunities in the situation, or we come to understand through the process more about our motives and fundamental concerns. But even when our fundamental motivation is stable, we refine by finding locally relevant expressions of it in the unfolding activity. As opportunities and situations change, so our local motives come into focus to meet the protean social realities we work within.

The importance of writing being part of ongoing interchanges is evident when we join some case after it has developed. To get "up to speed" we need to read the file, which gives the facts of the case, the facts of the participants, the positions each has staked out and elaborated, and the relationship forming among them—and the overall trajectory of the interaction. It often helps to have someone who has been part of the proceedings to this point to explain and interpret what is going on. Only with great and focused work can we attempt to undo any of the social facts and speech acts already accomplished in the file. Further, even with explanations from the prior participants, reading the file, is usually not enough to get fully up to speed, for which we need a couple of further turns in the back and forth. Equally, interlocutors need to see the moves the new person makes so they can evaluate what our intentions and modes of procedure are.

Unless we have some reflective understanding of our motives, the unfolding nature of situations, and our changing participation in a dynamic situation, we are at risk of getting locked into a set of motives and stances that are less productive and may not achieve our ends. A slavish following of what we believe is the right form for the situation or a slavish adherence to our first conception of our motives can lead to an unfortunate trajectory of interaction that leaves participants at an impasse, or caught in an unproductive distracting side-issue. It is worth asking ourselves periodically what we really want from a situation, what will meet our needs and carry forward a productive interaction with our audiences and interlocutors.

With such an understanding we can think about whether a change of footing will create a more favorable ground for reframing the interaction, allowing parties to define new roles and stances, engaging in adjusted projects. This is where motives and genre meet. Each genre has implied motives, implied roles for the readers (what Bakhtin, 1986, called addressivity), and actions which represent the illocutionary force of the genre. Equally, our readers may have developed stances, attitudes, and resistant responses to the genres, roles, and stances we adopt. Accordingly a shift of those genres and understandings surrounding them on both sides may re-center the discussion on more productive grounds. Or combining multiple generic understandings within a single utterance, may invite greater complexity of response and understanding. The strategic understanding of how we may advance our interests and concerns in a situation is the subject of the next chapter.

CHAPTER 7

TEXT STRATEGICS

Traditional views of rhetoric have identified the key strategic action to be accomplished as persuasion—that is to bring the audience to agreement with the speaker's view or position. Such a strategic goal is appropriate to the arenas of judicial, parliamentary, and political decision within which rhetoric developed, and even to the arena of spiritual conversion and homiletics (to which rhetoric became extended in the early Christian period). When the goal is persuasion, the main vehicle is argument, to turn other minds in the desired direction.

However, the view presented in this book suggests a range of strategic written actions that may be accomplished in many arenas of activity, unfolding over time rather than in single moments of decision. A broader way of characterizing the goal of rhetoric is influence rather than persuasion. Influence only requires that other people act in some way that recognizes or responds to your utterance. A geologist need not have any degree of disagreement with another person to influence them by providing a detailed report on geologic stresses along a fault so that you can together estimate current risks. Nor does a homeowner need to argue with other neighborhood homeowners in a series of emails coordinating an annual clean-up drive that all are committed to by long-standing practice. The communicative work in either case is not to persuade someone to something they would not already have acceded to. The influence is to create conditions for successful outcomes by providing information or coordinating schedules.

In other cases, it may be that the desired influence is not to create agreement, but to create further divisions and differences with the interlocutor. A businessperson may wish to identify exactly where her concerns and interests differ from a business partner, so that they can renegotiate the terms of the agreement. People may wish to detail the idiosyncratic particulars of their lives, experiences, and emotions so that they may understand each other better or just enjoy sharing unusual events and perspectives. In a contentious situation a statement can be for the benefit of third parties to understand the choice they have in adopting different views or can be to instigate an opponent to an extreme action or statement. Influence is as various as human activities and the ways we have of participating in them so as to somehow affect the outcome. So to think strategically about writing, we need to be considering what outcome we are looking for and how our writing may help bring that about.

Even within the traditional realms of political deliberation sometimes the most effective writing actions are not those aimed overtly at persuasion, as anyone who has written an agenda for a committee is aware. The most effective action may not be to bring powerful arguments and evidence to a meeting, but to allow or disallow an item coming to a vote or to shape the form of the proposition to be voted on. At times even more powerful is to write the agenda so that before the contentious issue comes to the floor, a committee can report that it is undertaking a study to gather facts on a related issue, such that the contentious vote is tabled pending the report. Then when that report arrives, its facts serve to redefine the nature of the problem the committee is addressing. While there may be specific elements of persuasion and specific arguments given in the course of the process, the overarching goal is influencing the events and outcome.

THE CORE OF STRATEGIC WRITING

The underlying strategic question that brings together all these situations is:

> How through a speech act can I change the symbolic land-
> scape so as to change the field upon which others will act
> in order to assert my concerns, interests, contribution, or
> participation into the process or outcome?

This question turns attention from the internal beliefs held by audiences and interlocutors to the unfolding of a social process in which I interact with others. At times the desired influence may require that I change the beliefs or views of those around me, replacing or qualifying some previously held belief they have, but more often it simply means they have to recognize and accept the legitimacy of the speech act I have made. As a consequence of that acceptance, they then need to calculate my act into any further move they make.

Rhetorical strategy, so conceived, examines the unfolding social situation, and the effect of any symbolic intervention in moving the situation forward. Rhetoric then attends as much to who is witnessing and paying attention to what I and others are saying as much as what is specifically said. In looking at what has been said, what I might say, and how others might take it up, as a rhetor I move from reading and anticipating minds as viewing what is visibly in the social field, including the unfolding intertext into which the new text will be inserted. While the strength, size, and effectiveness of some speech acts may depend on how it resonates with the dispositions, beliefs, sentiments, and interests of the relevant audiences, it is as important as to attend to the nature and rules of the game one is engaged in, and the particular forcefulness of moves in that game than to pull out all the operatic stops.

By identifying the act one desires to accomplish, the rhetor turns his or her energies toward what conditions need to be met for the act to be felicitous or successful in the particular situation. Further, the rhetor considers how you can make the act as forceful, well-defined, identifiable, and solid as possible, accomplishing its tasks as strongly as possible and standing for as long as it needs, for all the purposes and auditors it needs to. Again, this directs attention toward the evolving landscape on which influence will be asserted, the unfolding actions of others, and the social rules, expectations and values that define acceptability, compelling force, and evaluation that will influence the fate of the speech act. This further directs attention to the way a successful speech act will then inhibit or support others to do what they wish in its wake.

THE CRUCIAL ORDINARINESS AND LACK OF CONTENTIOUSNESS OF MOST WRITING

Most of the writing we carry out in the world is not in opposition to any particular others, nor to displace any beliefs or commitments people may have. Indeed, displacing someone's existing beliefs or commitments is difficult to accomplish. It is easier to tell someone something new than to get them to change something they already believe, even though for reasons of social harmony they may appear to acquiesce at the moment. Even if they agree with you, you may find it is only on a detail rather than with a deep-seated understanding and acceptance of your view. You may well find old beliefs persist and resurface later. This persistence of beliefs, attitudes, and perspectives, in fact should be expected, for after all, personal experiences, knowledge, and views are often long standing and integrated with an individual's way of looking at life. How often do a few words by someone else significantly change the deeply structured patterns and networks of our thought and perceptions? Such moments are rare enough to be considered remarkable—and even many of those cases involve simply the articulation of existing inchoate impulses ready for crystallization.

Only in highly structured situations like courts, parliaments, or scientific disciplines with regular procedures for coming to communal decisions does effective changing of minds or at least compelling acquiescence to the communal judgment happen with frequency. In such domains there are well known forms of compelling evidence, acceptable lines of reasoning, publicly recognized evaluative criteria, and public accountability for one's ultimate position. Contention to be effective must stay within well-defined rules particular to the domain—the rules of evidence in experimental psychology are different from that in ethnographic sociology, let alone high-energy physics. And those are all very far from the rules of evidence and testimony in court, so that the knowledge of these fields to be admissible in court requires new procedures and transformation of form, evidence, and authority. Further, even in those domains of structured judgment, individuals whose claims lose and no longer stand with any communal force still may maintain belief that they were right even as they are dragged off to jail or fail to have their grants renewed and works cited. It is the institutional and collective judgment carried out through institutional procedures that has the final judgment, not the state of mind of particular individuals.

More commonly writing is carried out within mutually agreed upon activities that do not depend on agonistic struggle. We write to participate within systems and organizations, establish relations, carry out responsibilities, facilitate conjoint work, build bonds and relations over time, assert identity and establish self-esteem within communities, entertain each other, or share common passions. Within such activities we do not displace any social facts that others have asserted and successfully established; we rather attempt only to create our own new social facts. We make speech acts, and only rarely attempt to undo the speech acts of others. And in making our speech acts we create the occasion and resources for others to act.

Creating a webpage describing our collection of antique phonographs may serve many functions in sharing nostalgia, amusing others with quirky aspects of history we have found in our avocation, displaying our pride in our collection, raising our esteem among aficionados, engaging young people in the history of technology, or in supporting scholarship in industrial history and cultural studies. We may even be trying to create a market in these artifacts and attract people to our antique offerings or catalog of reproductions. Yet none of these displace what anyone else does, except in the sense that others might have to carry out their similar activities in a more crowded landscape, which is not necessarily a bad thing for them, as it increases the overall traffic and adds resources for their own activities.

Writing a newsletter for our community association lets people know who is doing what, builds bonds of joint recognition and action, and provides information to allow people in the community to participate. It brings events, people, activities, and possible cooperations to people's attentions, thereby making their lives a bit richer. Only when the town council entertains a zoning motion that threatens some in the community might there be arguments for and against—and then that rhetorical agonism most likely would be directed toward a council meeting or an election, where a decision will be made. Otherwise, the task is building new things and not opposing anything already on the discursive landscape.

When one applies to a college, or for a grant, or any other competitive situation, one presents the best representation of one's own work and accomplishment in ways that will be credible and stand as an accurate and truthful statement. One tries to make as strong a speech act as possible that will not topple over because one of its fundamental props is found faulty. One typically is not in the business of undermining the attempted speech act of competitors, but only in having one's act standing taller, larger, and more in the correct spot for the purposes and criteria of the judging institution.

Even in filing an application for a building permit that meets all regulations and requires no exceptions, one is creating speech acts that carry forward bureaucratic regulation—populating the city records with information to be evaluated and used by others in monitoring, planning, collecting taxes, and other daily actions. Likewise sending holiday greetings to friends keeps alive social networks as well as shares participation in seasonal rituals. All these quotidian texts expand the intertext within which others operate and thereby create more facts to attend to in making their choices and asserting their actions.

THE PLACES OF INFORMATION AND REASONING

In completing each of these acts there are expected things to be said and information presented, and other things that would appear inappropriate. The information needed for a tax form would be inappropriate for a holiday greeting, even if your friends were tax examiners or your tax accountant. That is for another time and place—and another document.

Each genre and its related social activities call for specific kinds of information, reasoning, and sentiments—which in classical rhetorical terms would be called *topoi* or places. They are places the text might visit in carrying out its work. While a *topus* or topic can be thought of as something mentioned in the text, it also attaches the text to something in the world, audience's emotions, speaker's character, or other texts. It then mobilizes, builds on or transforms our relation to the *topus* brought to mind. Thus in a sense each *topus* the text visits attaches the reader to something outside the text, which is brought to bear on the action of the text. Thus in asking for a personal loan a person may remind the potential lender of long friendship and trust, to recall the borrower's reliability and responsibility and also to invoke a special trust that the borrower would not violate. In visiting these issues the borrower attempts to take the lender mentally to these places and activate them as relevant. On the other hand if the lender holds strongly to the adage that loans spoil friendships and that one should never loan to a friend unless you are ready to lose both money and friend, taking the communication to the relationship might suggest the opposite reaction. You don't want to go there, as we commonly say.

As each of our words index some reality, they each take the minds of others to places familiar or uncomfortable, known in detail or unknown and filled with specters—whether fearful or entrancing. Most often we just bring each other facts that make visible the world in which our speech act takes place and which fulfills the conditions that need to be met for the action to be successfully complete. Thus for parents to enroll their child in a local school, they must provide basic data, specified on a form with fields we must fill in, such things as names of child and parents, address of residency, emergency contact person and information, age and prior schooling of the child, vaccination and other health history. These establish within the school's documentary system realities relevant for the school's treatment of the application and then the actual child once the child enters the school door. The form requires the parents to visit each of the appropriate places and bring back the relevant token of that reality. Further, there needs to be confirmation of those indexed realities, which is often intertextual, requiring back-up documents, such as a birth certificate, vaccination certificate, and proof of address. While these documents may be accepted on their face in the moment, they of course each link up to other documentary systems, and their validity within those documentary systems could be tested. Even more forcefully, filling out the form directly links this current application with active intertextual links the system may have, such as initiating a request to the child's prior school to send records or linking the address into the city residency and taxpayer base. Parents may even have fears that there will be linkages to documentary systems where they would not want to appear, such as the immigration service, the taxation system, or a justice system with active warrants. Only if they know enough about the system and there are explicit privacy policies that limit uses and linkages, can these specters about the documentary realities invoked be laid to rest.

A second strategic set of questions is that of places—the places you enter and stand on along with the places you bring in as part of your speech act:

a. Where do you want to enter the documentary system and where not?
b. What place within it do you want to inhabit, act, or take a stand?
c. What kind of action in that place do you want to create to reach your ends?
d. What other places do you want to index and invoke at the place you are taking your stand or creating your act?

Let me go through each of these four more carefully.

A. THE PLACES YOU DECIDE TO ENTER OR NOT ENTER

The parents who fear filing information with the school because they don't know where that information is going may or may not be justified in their fears, depending on state and local regulations about the articulation of information between systems and the actions of local officials, but they are correct in understanding that any time you write or have inscribed information within a system you are creating a presence within it and with any other systems that may intersect with it. You are entering the places of that literate, documentary activity system by asserting a presence. As literate systems have spread and become pervasive, some people try to keep their entire presence or some aspect of their lives outside of the encompassing documentary system. As the tax system and its monitoring of transactions has grown, it has produced a grey economy of transactions conducted "off the books" in cash or barter or "off-shore" so as not to be visible to national tax documentation. Companies keep themselves private so as not to be subject to the scrutiny of stockholders and the various agencies that protect the rights of stockholders. Most people do not write letters to the editor or engage in the public sphere of politics, except perhaps when they are asked to be an anonymous respondent in a poll or a voting booth, and even then they may be hesitant. People, as well, know once they announce themselves to a charitable organization by giving a donation or putting themselves on a mailing list, they are opening themselves up to persistent solicitations.

The core of privacy issues as they have emerged on the internet concerns which documentary systems inscribed information will go to and to what extent it will stay within the ambit for which it was initially inscribed, whether as an email to an individual, an order to a commercial seller, a comment in a password protected chat room, or a posting to a publicly accessible blog. Given the extensiveness and publicness of electronic networks, however, it is difficult to identify what the bounds are of the world you are communicating with. In the print world only a small group of self-selected individuals published their work, usually on a limited range of issues through a crafted public voice. In a world as comprehensively documented and inscribed in every aspect as ours, however, it has even become a form of ideological, individualistic commitment of some to "live off the grid."

Most of us choose most of the time not to enter into most documentary systems except those we feel compelled to do so by such strong social forces as schooling, government regulation, community expectations, or employment. Indeed most of them are of no interest to us, unless we ourselves are programmers of a particular computer language, macramé weavers, aficionados of Raymond

Carver mysteries, animal rights activists, or engaged in scriptural interpretation. We are so unaware of most of the literate spheres of activity that go on around us that we would be surprised to find out how many of them there are and how extensive some of them may be

We define our lives, interests, and activities by those social groups we selectively engage with. The immediate compelling relationships of those we engage with daily face-to-face have always been primary in shaping our lives, but increasingly over the centuries these have been supplemented, enriched, and encased within documentary systems that link us up with people at a distance of time and space. While sitting around at night by candlelight and then by electric light, we came to read books, write letters, and now withdraw to separate computer terminals—connecting each individual in the family up with different collective worlds that may affect vocabulary, manner of dress and self-presentation, beliefs, attitudes, commitments, and actions.

While the literate communities we connect up often have to do with the chances of personal acquaintants, community affiliations, and local institutional arrangements of school, church, and government, over the last several centuries communication technologies have opened up increasingly greater opportunities for elective engagement—starting with the circulation of books, creation of periodicals, and the formation of public libraries. Initially our worlds grew mostly as readers, as consumers of the products of a small group of authors, who were perceived as extraordinary. While some limited networks of publications had more of a symmetrical sharing of roles, such as in special interest group newsletters, only with the emergence of the internet and associated forums of digital interaction (e-lists, self-sponsored websites, chatrooms, blogs, tweets and whatever else will be coming along) were fuller ranges of participation available to most people. This proliferation of opportunities makes the issue of choice of where one wishes to become engaged a serious question for more and more people.

B. THE PLACE YOU WANT TO INHABIT, ACT, TAKE A STAND ON, OR BE NOTICED

Even when we have interests in participating in specific networks of communication, we must make a commitment of time and energy to visit the places where people engage in our chosen domain of activity, identify and select relevant texts to read, and start to make sense of that world. It is even a further commitment to think we might have anything to add and then to begin to frame our own contributions. We make a further commitment when we decide to make ourselves visible by sending the letter, by pushing the submit button, by seeking publication of a notice in the local newspaper. In becoming visible we cause ourselves to wonder what kind of figure we will cut, whether people will pay attention, what they think of what we contribute, whether we will create negative views or even get ourselves in trouble. Thus we need to become strategic about exactly where and when we appear.

A strong statement in the wrong time and place will not be attended to because people's minds and energies are going in different directions and are not primed to attend appropriately to the statement. Within legal systems papers have to be filed in timely ways to the right office, otherwise they are rejected or ignored. Less technically determined, a letter to a newspaper editor about an evolving political issue a month ago will likely not be published, or sending the political comment to the entertainment editor will be equally ineffective. We must identify a time and place when our words have a reasonable possibility of having the hoped-for attention and effect.

C. THE KIND OF ACTION YOU WANT TO TAKE AND THE PRESENCE YOU WANT TO ESTABLISH

In conjunction with deciding the appropriate moment for entry, you need to decide the particular form of action you want to take, which then suggests the genre you choose to write in and thus the way you will make your presence known. Actually these choices are not distinct and sequential, as the available genres suggest the kinds of presences and action, and the kinds of presence carry with them consequences for genre and action. Each moment creates constraints of appropriacy because your readers will be primed to accept, recognize, or be interested in only a range of actions, genres, and presences they perceive as appropriate or germane or meaningful to the moment. No matter how important a student may feel that the professor should understand the deep background of personal ambivalence the student has toward the subject matter of the course, the instructor may quite likely wonder where the answer to the question assigned is. The instructor may also wonder whether he or she really ought to be this student's intellectual therapist, or more properly focus on being a history instructor.

On the other hand you may have a number of different ways of responding or carrying forward an activity that would be considered relevant, meaningful, and useful. Several genres could serve to introduce your fellow board members to a new approach to building membership in your organization. You could describe a future scenario of a vibrant organization with new groups of members, you could analyze current member trends, you could review recent other attempts and why they have failed, or you could narrate the success story of a similar organization. Each approach invokes a genre and defines whether you present yourself as a visionary, a careful analyst, a strategic thinker, or an inspirational motivator.

Equally with each choice of action, genre, and presence you are making a series of choices about stance toward the ongoing conversation, issues, and activities. Your proposal for increasing membership can express anxiety about the current situation or evoke empathy for an unmet need. You can have contempt, agnosticism, or respect for previous proposals. You can see some facts as needing attention and others as insignificant and not worth mentioning. The stance you take will resonate with or alienate your readers, will create a perspective for your readers or distance you from the perspectives they are committed to, will influence them and strengthen the force of the action or will undermine how much they are willing to accept your act at face value, rather than attributing hidden motives to you.

Thus in engaging in a discussion, you are attempting to stake out some ground on an ongoing landscape of communication and activity that your readers will recognize. You need to be able to define the ground in a way the readers will recognize and place your attempted act so that they will see it fitting, acceptable, appropriate, and meaningful.

D. THE RESOURCES YOU WANT TO DRAW INTO YOUR SPACE

Too often we think of texts simply as written within their own spaces—as though they were fictions floating apart from other worlds. But even fictions draw on the readers' experiences and emotions in the world to create power within the fictive worlds. Even more, everyday texts draw on and bring together realities outside the text to establish their relevance and force in specific circumstances. Presenting demographic facts about unequal healthcare accessibility is not just a rhetorical trick to make a point; it indexes social realities that need addressing. It says the world demands the kind of attention being given in this text. The text's invocation of these facts then makes the text and author accountable for the accuracy of the representation—that those statistics are well gathered and are germane to the issue at hand. Similarly tying texts to files of information on a patient's case or a long standing discussion of philosophers locates the text in on going exchanges, but also gives the weight of prior discussions to the text at the same time as holding the text accountable to those discussions.

A text representing the world and taking action in it is only as strong as the ground it is anchored to and the strength of the anchors. That is, the claimed representation of conditions in the world must accountably be supportable. An application for a loan identifies the applicant as a person with a credit history—which will be checked against the files of banks and loan institutions. If the name is false, the claim of employment is inaccurate, there is no history of financial transactions, or the transactions are flawed to indicate lack of creditworthiness, the application will fail.

In some situations the expectations of the genre necessary to take action are so specific that they address all the conditions necessary to complete the act—and also thereby all the resources that need to be brought to bear, indexed, and accountably certified. At the extreme are bureaucratic forms that dictate all the information to be provided, the appropriate form and order in which they need appear, intertexts of data bases and files that confirm and provide expanded details on the reported information, and signed statements making one accountable under legal penalty for the accuracy and truthfulness of the information provided. The bureaucratically determined requirements of the regulated action walk you through all the places you must visit and report on, identify the kinds of details you must use to index the realities and how far you need to go into them—and no further (limited by the size of the space and the specific items requested). Further, the form locates your assertions within institutional and informational resources, activates all necessary supplementary materials, orders them in a way that facilitates their processing by the receiving agency, defines your stance as an applicant or other subaltern to the institutional and organization body, and makes you accountable for your role in the process.

Even in somewhat less compulsory genre situations the expected organizations of texts identify the places you should be taking the discussion, the information and resources you need to represent, and the kind of reasoning you should be doing with these resources. If you are considering for an urban civic blog the impact of new policing procedures, you must first establish the policies you are talking about, when they have been put in place, and some sense of the community situation before and after. Then you might take the discussion to a number of places, but each of those places must be demonstrably related to public impacts, consequences, and responses to the policy. You may take the discussion to crime statistics, a description of main street on a weekend night, the mood of people in one of the more troubled parts of town, the talk in a local gang hangout, the concerns of parents expressed at a community meeting, a press conference held by the local civil liberties organization—or any of a number of places where consequences of and reactions to the policy may be seen. You could take the discussion to state laws and the federal constitution, with scholarly discussion of what is permitted and what violates fundamental law. You may even take the discussion to a scene from a popular television crime show or movie.

Each choice of place you take the discussion carries with it a kind of reasoning. Legal discussion requires you to examine legal material through legal reasoning. Listening to community groups raises issues of public belief, interests, and reactions which need to be discussed. Reference to entertainment requires you to be aware of the difference between fiction and reality and possibly also the role of media-represented beliefs and images in affecting or contrasting with realities. Not only are you accountable for the reasoning of that location, but the reasoning that ties that location to the issue you are considering. Also typically at the end of such a piece, you would return to the realities of your town.

You may even create hybrid genres that take the discussion to strange places. You could take your consideration of the policing policy to a science fiction fantasy to demonstrate a dystopic or utopic future that would result from the policy and related approaches, or you could create a computer game or cartoon to mock the impulses behind the policy. But still you need to be sure the audience understands the fundamental linkage of this kind of representation to the issue at hand.

The contrast between the closed example of the loan application and the open-ended one of the civic blog also highlights differences in depth the places indexed may be examined. In the loan application it is only important that the representation be good enough—what is asked for, accurate, appropriate, truthful. More would only get in the way. Once you have given what is needed for approval, no one needs or wants to hear any more. In the civic discussion there is no clear ending to how deeply you might want to go, where the discussion would lead. The strength of the act you want to build may be limited by the information you can find out, the amount of concern the community has, and the tolerance and attention span of your audience, but there is nothing predetermined in the genre or basic action to tell you when enough is enough and when more is no longer useful or even welcome. Chapter 9 of this volume provides more details on managing representations of the world and the intertext in your writing

Writing a text is creating a new object on an intertextual landscape and populating that text with representations and meanings and to animate those meanings as the reader engages with the text (see Chapter 11 of this volume). The rhetorical influence of the text is a consequence of readers' engagement with these texts transforming their view of the social, material, and literate worlds of their future actions. The fundamental strategic question is how you can best populate the intertextual landscape with new objects to gain the influence you hope for, to meet your own interests, needs, concerns, or creative visions. Selecting the most effective places to inhabit, building engaging landmarks that call attention to those things you select for others to be aware of, and then creating ways of thinking about the place and objects in the course of text are the strategic means of influencing thought and social processes. The remaining chapters of this volume pursue how one can bring these textual objects into being in their most complete and effective form.

CHAPTER 8

EMERGENT FORM AND THE PROCESSES OF FORMING MEANING

The writer's emergent strategic judgments about construal of situation, places of engagement, effective actions, relevant resources, and stances contain many implications for the form the text will take, both at the level of genre and of details that make a particular text. Strategic choices shape what aspects of the situation and the particular object of concern will be represented, how other contexts will be brought to bear, and how the writer will attempt to engage the minds and spirits of the readers. The text is the form into which all these considerations are crystallized and dynamically conveyed to the readers. That form must be recognizable and meaningful to the readers to allow them to make sense of what the writer is doing and then act upon it appropriately.

WELL-KNOWN GENRES AND SEDIMENTED FORM

Sometimes a writer may be able to characterize the situation and action in well-defined, stable, non-mistakable generic terms—now it is time to send out an announcement of the upcoming party or now is the time to write a letter threatening legal action unless the bill is paid. Each of these has well known characteristics with a certain limited range of choices, known to those who regularly practice them. If a writer has difficulties with either, it is likely either because of lack practice in the genre or because exceptional circumstance put some strain on genre expectations. Further, each genre places specific requirements on what must be accomplished through particular textual means, no matter how inventive the writer is in carrying out some of the textual functions. So whether the writer expresses a festive and welcoming atmosphere with pictures of balloons or a joking excuse for the party, or expresses dignity with formal calligraphy on parchment, the invitation needs to identify who is invited, who is doing the inviting, the nature of the event, date, time, place, some indication of the dress or formality, and perhaps directions and a request for response. This is true whether the invitation is publicly posted on a lamppost or personally addressed on a specially printed card. Equally the letter threatening legal action needs to identify the recipient and sender, the agreement and obligation, the date and place for response, and other details that indicate the legal consequences. In most cases legal threat needs to be cast in sober legal business letter format to be taken seriously; having it sent by an attorney further emphasizes the seriousness. These well-known genres have created packages of situations, actions, resources, author stances, and audience roles all wrapped up in well-known forms. All you need do is fulfill the requirements of the form and deliver the package.

As the action situation and the genre choice emerge, some writing decisions follow quite directly. Of course much substantial textual work still is to be done in selecting appropriate and effective words to fulfill the requirements as well as other related, non-textual work. Before you finish writing the invitation, you need to arrange for a place to hold the party and a commitment for its availability at the time, as well as to make sure that you have the funds for the promised entertainment and refreshments, and so on. Similarly in writing the legal letter you need to gather together all the relevant legal documents and agreements to know what details to include, how defensible your position is, and how to properly threaten within this particular legal situation. If you want to add legal muscle, you need to hire a lawyer, and the law firm has had to develop a suitably powerful looking letterhead. All of these other actions will bear on how the text will appear, what specific language and information is used, and how the text will be interpreted.

THE WORK TO DO WITHIN GENRES: MAKING OF MEANING

In working within stable, familiar genres you would do well to look to previous examples and existing genre-specific guidelines to know the formal requirements, what the readers will expect, and the choices that are likely to be effective. But you also need to look to the particulars of your situation to make the text do the specific work you need done in this case. For some genres simple fulfillment of requirements may be all that is needed. Submitting an order for a new product needs to be accurate and complete as to what is ordered, where it is to be shipped, how payment is to be made, and so on. It must be addressed and transmitted to a business that sells the product and can deliver it as requested, and you must have the authorization to order and make payment. Once you have presented this as clearly as possible in the most familiar and easily interpretable way, your job is done. Any extra information, attempt at humor or a personal touch, or political comment might confuse the business-client relationship.

On the other hand, you may need further work on the text beyond the required minimum. While sometimes a standard party invitation is enough, at times you may want to encourage participation or raise anticipatory joy by clever words, interesting graphics, personal photographs, or some other individualizing device. To do this successfully you need to go beyond the typical formal elements of the genre into the spirit of the event and the specifics of the situation. For a wedding invitation you might want to look into the values and dreams of the couple and the role of the partnership in their lives to provide clues as to what makes this celebration special. The standard legal letter, in the other example, may not be sufficiently threatening to be effective in a particular case, given what you know of the circumstances and the callous attitude of the offenders, so you may need to look into the offenders' vulnerabilities and fears to know what will spell trouble to them and get their attention. In both cases, nonetheless, the inventiveness remains within the expectations of the genre, though heightening its force.

Many genres have the expectation of novelty, originality, fresh thought, particular situational aptness or other invention even to fulfill successfully the basic requirements of the genre. The genre directs the character of the invention, points the writer toward particular kinds of work, and whets the readers' appetites for a particular kind of surprise. Jokes (unless they are in special categories of old and familiar jokes such as "groaners") require a surprise in the punchline, usually involving a pun, juxtaposition, incongruity, or other disruption of ordinary thinking—but it cannot be too shocking or sobering. While Op-ed columns in the newspaper are typically of a certain length, within a recognizable style, and about current events, yet each one is expected to present a fresh perspective on the events that show a special wisdom, insight, perspective, or knowledge that will stimulate the reader's thinking. To do this the columnist has to watch for interesting stories about which he or she has something fresh to say. Much of the work of writing such columns is in identifying events to talk about and the perspective from which to discuss them.

THE WORK OF ACADEMIC GENRES: LEARNING THROUGH PROBLEM SOLVING

Most student papers in fulfillment of university assignments similarly need to respond to an instructor's expectation of fresh thinking on the students' part, often specified and directed in the assignment. This fresh thinking typically will require the use of ideas and methods presented in the course and discipline, and will typically be based on reason and evidence, but will include some novel critical perspective, evaluation, analytical reasoning or other recognizable intellectual work. The student to succeed must not only recognize the general requirements of the assignment, but also the specific expectations of novel work added, to distinguish this paper from and above others in the class at the same time as being recognizably within the framework of the course and assignment.

In university settings student writing is often assigned to develop student analytical thinking, and ideally students and teachers enter into a productive dialogue about the disciplinary material, growing from students' engagement in the subject matter and the ideas being raised in the course. Academic genres, particularly in classroom or seminar settings, frequently have strong dialogic expectations—reprising ideas and materials already developed as part of the course as well as bringing fresh but appropriate external resources as part of the student's creative, critical, informed contribution. Furthermore, readers (or interlocutors in this educational dialogue) are usually looking for the organization, linkages and reasoning that provides evidence of a mind at work on disciplinary questions, using disciplinary resources and tools—that is, a mind that is being disciplined through the disciplinary task.

From this perspective, the genre the students are working in, directed by the prompt or assignment, becomes a problem space in which the students are learning by working through disciplinary issues using disciplinary tools and varieties of analytical, synthetic, and critical reasoning. The formulated argument of the paper then becomes both an expression of the student's answer to this problem and evidence of their thinking, reasoning, and learning.

GIVING SHAPE TO THOUGHT: THE PARADOXES OF FORM

In such assignments the disciplinary learning and the writing become inseparable, and the instructor is likely to evaluate and respond to the paper precisely as a piece of disciplinary work, revealing the student's disciplinary understanding. There is sometimes an even deeper reading of the student's development which can be evaluated and responded to, concerning the student's depth of engagement and commitment to the field and its fundamental intellectual perspectives. That is, sometimes the instructor may be looking for evidence that the student is not just displaying disciplinary reasoning—even novel, clever reasoning—as an acquiescence to the authority relations in the classroom, but that somehow the student has made the disciplinary perspective his or her own, has integrated disciplinary thinking into his or her own internally persuasive resources (to use Bakhtin's terms, 1981) as something to believe and use in viewing the world. While the indicators of that engagement may be fluid and task specific, they would indicate thought that extends beyond the immediate problem and the obvious resources as part of some further intellectual transformation within the student.

One of the regular challenges students have as writers, if they are indeed working from their own deeply internal thought, rather than thinking of the writing as simply an external set of forms and requirements to be fulfilled, is that they get lost in their thoughts and their writing may remain elliptical as internal thought often is (as described by Vygotsky, 1986.) Further, because student writers may have a sense that they know what they are talking out, the writing may not be intelligible to a differently minded audience. Because they have lived through an episode and may have multiple visceral memories of the situation, they may not share details necessary for others to picture and understand the situation. Certain personally important words may be used in idiosyncratic ways or with a force understood only by the author. So an important part of students learning to write for these situations is to expose and elaborate enough of their thought and experience so that their thought becomes intelligible to the reader.

These expectations about what might appear in the final paper raise paradoxes of internal processes and external production which riddle education as an enterprise, as educators evaluate external behaviors and products to determine students' internal development. Educators set challenging activities and establish responsive environments in order to foster internal development, and regularly make attributions about students' intellectual and emotional selves on the basis of their behaviors and products. These paradoxes are heightened in schooling because of the focus on the development of students' minds, but actually the tension between external form and internal thought runs throughout writing. Writing, as all language, is a vehicle to evoke meanings in other peoples' minds. Readers in turn believe that the thoughts they glean from a text had their origin in the mind of the writer. Even a pro forma social nicety or a lie must still be selected and thus thought. Yet what is transmitted are the words on paper or on the computer screen—an external object made of signs, which can be manipulated and evaluated as a formal construction. Nevertheless, the signs index thoughts entertained and projected by the writer and thoughts evoked in the readers, although the reader's thoughts may not match those projected by the writer.

The complexity and personality of thought leads to an indeterminacy and creativity in what the formal realization might be. But that formal realization requires that we work with forms and make choices about formal elements. That tempts us to treat writing on the purely formal level, for that is where skill seems to reside. Yet we are always engaged in the task of making meaning and wrestling with form to express that meaning.

BEING PRACTICAL ABOUT PARADOXES: BIDDING THE MUSE

One way to deal with these paradoxes of inner meaning and outer form is to wait for a moment of inspiration when one's perception of the situation, impulse for meaning, and sense of possible form crystallize in an intuitive sense. Such moments of writer's intuition can be very powerful and can direct writing strongly. Certainly a writer should cultivate the ability to identify and respect those moments when they appear, but their appearance at best will be sporadic and unpredictable. Most of our writing does not arise in the leisure that allows us to write poems only when the spirit moves us and the vision is clear. Even in that luxurious situation, such moments of illumination are more likely to strike if we are regularly at our keyboard or have pen in hand, struggling with meaning and form, at the altar of the muse, ready to recognize and transcribe when the muse visits us.

So what can we do until the muse arrives or even in the likely case the muse never visits? We can work from the outside in, or from the inside out, or moving back and forth.

FROM THE OUTSIDE IN: UNDERSTANDING THE MEANING OF FORM

For fairly stabilized genres in fairly stabilized social circumstances, models, guidelines, advice, instructions, or textbooks can tell us what to include, how it should be organized, how it should be expressed. These directive documents range from detailed instructions about how to fill out government forms, to collections of model letters, to reference books on how to write a scientific article, to self-help books on writing scripts for television. They may even lay out very specific technical requirements for specific fields, such as proper terminology and citation form for scientific articles in chemistry, or all the items that must be included for an application to be considered. Increasingly, especially in digital environments, templates are provided (and sometimes monitored) to identify (and sometimes compel) topics and information as well as to structure the presentation. Forms can even police our responses to ensure they are in the correct format. Although now machine monitoring of generic completeness is limited to fairly simple items in forms (name, address, etc.), we can only expect that this kind of structuring and monitoring will increase—including inspection of the content of more open-ended sections. In any event, even if such content expectations are not externally prompted, we can query ourselves and start to make lists of the kind of things expected in the document and specifics that we might want to include. Through such lists, notes, and outlines, the contents of texts can emerge and then be organized, giving us confidence and direction in what we say, even if we do not strictly adhere to this early planning.

Sometimes the guidance is more sketchy and open-ended, recognizing the differences of particular cases and the need for the creation of new meanings within the genre. This guidance may be more strategic identifying impulses or gists that need to be carried out or identifying larger sweeps of meaning. Such is the advice offered for scientific article introductions developed by John Swales (1990), that identifies a series of moves that a researcher needs to do to identify the rationale for a piece of research. One creates a research space by a series of moves that identifies a problem, establishes what prior research has been done in the literature and identifies a gap or opening in the research. Similar analyses have been done for other forms writing, identifying the usual set of moves in a genre, with the typical variations, additions, deletions, substitutions, and changes in sequence. These move analyses usually display a strategic logic in the selection and order of the moves, which are identified by examination of many real examples.

The tension between external form and the internal meaning-making suggests we take a somewhat sophisticated approach toward the formal requirements and practices typical in a situation. Models and guidance about specific contents, organization, appropriate language and phrasing, and other describable aspects of language put the appropriate tools of language at our fingertips, reminding us of the many things we already know or introducing us to new particulars that can extend our repertoire. But we also are helped by understanding the meaning to be conveyed that prompt these formal elements. Understanding the logic, the idea behind the formal requirements, first of all lets us know what we are doing, so we can direct our attention to the basic task of making meanings that fit the situation. The form does not displace the meaning, but helps us understand what kind of meanings we can create. Second, in moving us toward the underlying gist realized through the form, we can think about how to create the gist more forcefully and effectively. Third, if we understand what we are trying to accomplish in the genre in terms of detailed meaning making, we are freed to try to alternative means—while still keeping in mind readers' expectations. While at times we may have to write exactly in the prescribed form or our reader will not accept our information, we often have some freedom to try new things as long as we respect and pay attention to expectations—explaining how we will fulfill expectations in a different way, or explaining persuasively why those expectations may need to be modified.

As we understand the meaning potentials and interactional gists that may be achieved in a situation, we may then also see that we can evoke more complex sets of understandings within the situation. By bringing the clusters of understanding packaged in multiple sets of genres we can develop meanings that draw on and resonate with several domains of activity, knowledge, ideas, and actions. If we consider genres not as fixed forms but recognizable clusters of psycho-social understandings, we have the possibility of invoking rich complexes of understanding in making our points. Of course, this requires clarity and focus in what we are doing so these multiple domains reinforce rather than confuse each other. This is all the more reason we need to look deeply into the worlds genres exist in and the worlds created by them.

FROM THE INSIDE OUT: MIDWIVING EMERGENT MEANINGS

As discussed in previous chapters, our responses to situations are visceral and complex, bringing many resources to the task as a communicative situation takes shape. Whatever theory of internal language, intuitive judgment, subconscious or preconscious mind, affective thought, or brain architecture and dynamics one may hold, all views recognize that the resources and responses that give rise to our statements are only partially available to our conscious mind and planning. In forming utterances we act below our self-conscious monitoring of meaning production to tap deeper processes. Arranging our lives so as to make our deepest thought most available is an important part of our work as writers. We can identify our best time of day for writing and leave it open for writing without distractions. We can organize a conducive working environment and have our favorite coffee in our favorite mug. Developing rituals and routines that relax and focus our mind, or organizing daily work to begin with easier warm up activities, such as looking at necessary sources or reviewing the previous day's work are all part of the process of getting our mind in the right place to be receptive to our emerging thoughts. Such activities could be called prompting the mind, finding the right place to put your mind into, or assembling the right frame of mind—they all are forms of mental preparation.

Preparing the mind to write is not always easy, especially if the subject is challenging—intellectually, emotionally, socially, or technically. Such challenges may leave us with an uncertainty about whether we have something appropriate to say or whether we are capable of saying it. We may not feel comfortable and may resist committing ourselves to words (see Chapter 12 for elaboration of these psychological challenges). But we must assemble the courage to begin putting something on the page. Notes, outlines, plans, random sentences, free-writing journals are all low stakes ways to get the words flowing—not fully committing us to decisions, but yet producing something outside the self. Ideas may then begin to flow. Low-stakes writing can open some directions to take and even phrases to keep. For the rest the wastebasket and delete button are near at hand. At the very least we wind up with some text to look at, evaluate, modify, or replace with something better. Externalizaton reduces the cognitive overload of keeping everything floating in the head and perhaps decreases the confusion that occurs when juggling too many ideas at the margin of consciousness.

BACK AND FORTH: BETWEEN EXTERNAL
FORM AND INTERNAL IMPULSES

As we get text on a paper, our ideas take material shape, as a painting emerges from an empty canvas. The impulses to project meaning turn into particular words and sentences, inscribed contents, sequences of thought, and pieces of text organization. At the first level we may simply consider whether this is what we wanted to say and whether it is intelligible to others or could be said more effectively. But then we can see where it is headed—what is necessary to complete the thought or elaborate it to be more fully understood, and what next point needs to be addressed.

As the text emerges, thinking moves more and more from discovering what it is you want to say to craftsman-like working with the actual text. Even then, crafting text still can be a continuing process of discovery as you have to answer questions about how one part relates to another, or what is an accurate example or specification of an idea, or whether audiences will object and how objections can be addressed. As we construct the document we literally make meaning, articulating impulses and organizing them into a document that becomes the conveyer of that meaning. Work on the document sharpens the public meaning, which then becomes the words which we stand behind. In that process we need to keep questioning about how true that text is to our impulse—for only by that questioning can we maintain a commitment to your words. On the other hand, the written words become our commitment as we struggle with how to make them say what we want, thereby creating a more elaborated meaning.

DRAFTY DRAFTS AND INTERIM TEXTS

A writer works with the meaning as it emerges. This may mean you may come up with a key phrase but with no clear idea where it will fit within the text. Get it down. Or a paragraph explaining a key concept may be a good place to start, or a description of a key location, or a reminder list of some things you want to make sure you cover. If in a research article the research methods you employed are easiest to write, begin there. On any pieces of writing, the introduction is the hardest part. You could skip it at first or just try anything to warm up, with the knowledge that you can delete it, change it, or substitute something later once you see what the body of the text actually winds up saying.

As you build the first draft, it can be quite drafty, with much air flowing through it. If you have sections that are difficult to address or which require further research or other activities, then you can skip them over, but do leave as many words as you can to guide you when you return to fill in the holes. When you first begin writing, it does not even have to be a draft of the final text. You can write some interim document, such as a freewrite journal or a description of the materials you have available, just to get your thoughts and plans out. Many kinds of projects require different documents at various points long before the final document gets drafted; the interim documents get the writers to a position to be able to write the final document. For example, major research projects may start with a brief proposal long before the research is done. Reading notes on related studies may capture important points for the new study or identify important procedures. Collecting information, whether from experiments, surveys, or archives, produces a variety of texts, notes, data documents, or files. Rearranging and displaying the information in tables, narratives, graphics and other formats can help make sense of them. Then analysis may produce a whole different generation of documents. Short interim presentations of work in progress for supervisors, colleagues, or sponsoring organizations can help clarify actions, thinking, and results to this point. While all these may be written long before final articles or books, they help the writer think through the project, figuring out what to say and what material to include. Phrasing, descriptions, and even whole sections that will find their way into final documents emerge. Often people writing large projects find it useful to publish shorter articles that become the basis of larger books.

If you trust the process, meaning and form will gradually emerge over the long period to produce a text that crystallizes your meaning. Trusting the dialogue between yourself and the emerging text can give you courage to face the uncertainty about how the page will be filled and what will fill it. This dialogue is enriched by engagement with the materials one is writing about and with others interested and knowledgeable on the subject. Too often in schooling we view each text as a one-time effort to be produced in a limited time span, with few texts and other humans around us. Outside school, we are more likely to write as part of an ongoing interaction with others, so that we develop our thoughts, positions and actions in each exchange. The process is ongoing and being caught up in it is the means by which we produce texts for it. It is rare that a full and crisp vision will impel the writer from the beginning. Rather we must learn to take courage from a process driven by our best efforts and deepest impulses to communicate. We can do no more. Trust the process.

CHAPTER 9

MEANINGS AND REPRESENTATIONS

A form in itself is a gesture toward a social interaction, but it contains little meaning in itself beyond the gesture. Occasionally that is enough, simply registering a social action, like saying hello, acknowledging receipt of a previous message, or signaling compliance with a request. But most social actions benefit from saying more, offering more meaning evoked through the contents. It is the contents that engage the mind of a reader, providing desired information or exciting the reader's thinking or evoking a shared perspective on the world or provoking outrage and action. This chapter provides some ways to think about the contents to select and how to represent them. The next chapter will provide some thoughts on how to bring these pieces together to create a total picture and a journey for the reader.

A PLACE FOR EVERYTHING AND EVERYTHING IN ITS PLACE

We know that if we are looking for specific kinds of information, we go to specific documents. If we want to know the ingredients for a dish, we check a recipe in a cookbook. If we seek information on voter preferences we check polls available in newspapers and political websites. If we want information about the most recent findings in microbiology, we go to the research articles of the field.

Each genre is associated with certain kinds of contents made available to or directed toward particular kinds of readers. As we write for each genre, we need to keep those expectations in mind, usually with the intention of fulfilling those expectations for those who will consult or read the documents. If we don't fulfill expectations we have some explaining to do or costs to pay. Some genres are highly restrictive. Any failure to include any of the required information in an application may lead to immediate rejection—and perhaps even a web application form will refuse to process it. Further, that information must be of the precise form expected, such as an address according to street, house and apartment number, city and state. A florid description of the charming house and how you might identify it by its distinguishing character would not work here, though it might be appropriate for the directions sent for a party.

Other genres may have more open expectations, but still some things in some forms would be clearly inappropriate. Information appropriate for an architectural proposal would not fit within a love letter, and the contents of neither would fit in a financial audit report. Each has its appropriate contents of interest and concern to its appropriate audience, a concept described by Bakhtin as a chronotope (1981)—the time and space each genre is placed in along with the appropriate scenery, actors, and actions. He uses the example of a Greek romance, but it is equally appropriate to a laboratory report that tells of several time places—the events carried out in the laboratory by the scientist through a method and apparatus, the story of what happens to the material placed under the experimental conditions, a framing story of what the discussion has been in the scientific literature and how this study intervenes in the discussion, and ultimately an emerging picture of what happens recurrently in the world as revealed by the findings of this and related studies. Each level of the story has its typical settings, time frames, actors, and events. Further, each level has a structured relation to each of the other levels of chronotope in the research report: the scientist's actions seek results relevant to the scientific discussion by designing an experiment which produces findings that contribute to a general picture of the operations of nature.

Sometimes seemingly inappropriate material can be brought into a genre, but it requires some specific warrant and some discursive work to legitimate its presence—diary material on the front page of a major newspaper would need to be justified as evidence in a serious political or financial scandal, unless the readers were to then decide this newspaper was turning into a tabloid scandal sheet. Perhaps a science writer could include a description of a flower-crowded garden at the beginning of a popular article on plant genetics, but only if the writer made clear connections to the article's exposition of its subject, such as connecting the varieties of flower colors, sizes, and shapes to genetic mechanisms determining such variety. But in a more professional research article in a scientific journal, a writer could probably not be able to justify such an aesthetic description no matter how hard the writer worked.

The genre chosen sets expectations of what needs to be included. Conversely, awareness of the kinds of information and ideas to be transmitted to particular audiences can suggest the appropriate genre to bring together and convey the message. Examining examples of genres you are considering can help you identify what the information expectations, the forms of representing the information, the level of detail and precision, and the uses made of the information—as well as the underlying need or justification for that information. Of course you must then look into the logic of what you are saying, and what particular needs your argument or task or subject calls for. At the intersection of your subject and the expectations of the genre you may be able to identify what you need, what your readers will expect, and the quality of the information you should provide.

WHERE AND HOW TO GET INFORMATION

But then there is still the question of where the information comes from and how to find it. Some genres carry specific expectations of procedures and standards for gathering and selecting the material, and may even require accounts of how the key material was collected. Research articles typically include explicit methodological narratives to provide warrant for and means of interpreting the information reported. Often, as well, they imply accounts of which concepts were selected and why, what articles were considered important to discuss, and which facts were important to consider.

In a typical school situation, the sources of information are often well defined by the textbook or assigned readings. If the teacher wants the students to seek additional materials from the library or from conducting a laboratory experiment, interviews, survey, or other research the teacher usually will be specific about the sources and procedures. Outside of school we may equally be expected to follow specific procedures for locating and selecting information, and then how we represent it in the text. Journalists, for example, are trained to gather facts from the courthouse, police briefings, interviews, informants, public records, and other accepted journalistic sources. Even in domains not shaped by such professional standards, writers are faced with the problem of which information to include and what are appropriate ways to get and confirm that information. If we are complaining to a seller about prices we have been billed, having the exact amount billed, the original invoice, the invoice number, its date, as well as the exact amount will make your case stronger, as will a cancelled check or credit card bill. If we are claiming a discrepancy with an advertised price, then having the details that appeared in the original and, along with the date and place of the advertisement, and even a photocopy of the ad will provide evidence for the claim. Some personal messages, of course, rely primarily on memories and feelings, but looking over photos of the past few days of vacation, or even the business cards of the restaurants visited, might help bring back a lot of strong feelings and specific memories that could give some force to a personal letter or a travel blog.

Awareness of the information typical of a genre and the procedures by which that information is accessed is important to help you know what to include, what should drive your choices, and where you can find what you need. It also lets you know the standards of the field or domain, to make sure the material you include is respected, trusted, and accepted by your readers. In certain fields evidence must be collected by proper experimental procedures defined by the field, and for which you must be trained. Introduction of new evidence, unusual collection methods, or different reasoning from evidence to conclusions will require extra work to justify the novelty and persuade the readers of legitimacy of the procedure. If professional journalists are discovered to have deviated from the procedures of their profession, they are at risk of being deemed incompetent or unethical. If journalists make an alternate choice, as did the new journalists of the 1970s in the U.S —such as Tom Wolfe and Norman Mailer—or more recently political bloggers, they need to do work to justify that unusual choice and its validity, and run the risk of rejection. But that new form of work may also create new genres and evidentiary expectations.

ONTOLOGY AND EPISTEMOLOGY

The kinds of information appropriate to each genre establish the world to be considered by that genre. That information represents and points to objects and events in the world beyond the text, and thus indicates the ontology of the genre. What is represented in genres that circulate among a social group identifies what objects and events are valued and worth paying attention to by the group; conversely, those things not represented are not visible to the group's discussions, considerations, calculations, evaluations, or negotiation of accuracy. Any change in what can be made visible in the genres circulated in a social group or how it is made visible changes the group's ontology.

Further, expectations for the kind of information to be used to represent the objects and events and how that information is to be collected carry with them deeper considerations about how we can know and represent the world, what modes of knowing and representing are reliable and significant, and how our collections and representations index the world (that is, how they point to aspects of the world and what they tell us about the world). Generic expectations also define what methods of collection and representation are not allowable as faulty, misleading, imprecise, uncertain, or otherwise discrediting. Such considerations of how the text can come to represent knowledge of the world through the collection and representation of evidence operationally define the epistemology of the text and the group.

As a writer communicating with any social group, it is worth being aware of the readers' ontologies and epistemologies, whether or not you share their views. Often professional training in a discipline or profession is precisely an induction into the shared ontologies and epistemologies of the field. If there are explicit discussions about the ontologies and epistemologies of the field you are writing for, it may be of value to look into them, particularly if you are a stranger to the field, but do remember that sometimes these discussions are written by philosophers outside the field seeking normative guidelines that do not necessarily reflect the actual ontologic and epistemic practices or orientations of insiders. On the other hand, many insider discussions about ontology and epistemology often go by other names. Often books for neophytes and students can be very enlightening about what the field attends to, what it considers the right way to learn about the world of interest, and how that evidence from the world should be best represented.

Many scientific fields have extensive methodological discussions of credible ways of gathering evidence and ways to evaluate the evidence so gathered. They have discussions about what objects are properly the concern of a field and what belong to other fields, as well as what appearances are not appropriate to the field and what common sense ways of looking are not really accurate by disciplinary standards. Fields also often discuss or contend over the appropriate way to represent information gathered about the world so as to enter into the reasoning and calculation of the field. Each domain has its appropriate forms of representation. For example, in ancient days, taxes were collected directly in kind from agricultural produce, so that one would have to offer every tenth bushel of wheat or every tenth cow to the authorities. Accounting of these taxes were in terms of the produce. But modern taxes are now accounted through the local currency in quantitative form, so that if you were paid through food and lodging, you would have to convert that into its cash equivalent to be reported on the tax forms. In some fields results need to be presented as quantitative data of the sort that can be manipulated and evaluated through various statistical procedures. Some fields favor theory-driven graphs of energy levels, aggregating many trials. Typically in historical fields, specific historical actors need to be identified and evidentiary documents need to be identified and discussed to establish specific actions, intentions, and beliefs. In some areas of ethnographic social science research, identities of people need to be kept hidden, although detailed accounts of their social circumstances may be elaborated. Over time fields also change their modes of representation as new theories become important and new data collection devices are used. These modes of representation make the data or evidence available for reasoning, evaluation, and calculation in the ways characteristic of the field. If the information is not represented in the proper form, the readers will have a hard time working and reasoning with it.

If you are writing as an insider, readers will expect you to have internalized and to adhere to the epistemologies and ontologies of the field (or at least one of the several that may exist within a more tolerant multi-perspectival field), and if you vary you will have to provide to your colleagues principled and persuasive reasons (themselves within the values of the field) to reconsider their epistemologies and ontologies. Not only professions and research fields have such ontologies and epistemologies. Religious communities also teach its adherents to attend to certain emotional or spiritual experiences or certain texts that are core parts of epistemologies and ontologies. Sports fans also have things they agree are worth their attention, how those things should be properly known, and what is a distraction from or diminution of the sports experience.

As an outsider to any group, it is also important to attend to the ontologies and epistemologies of people you are communicating with—starting with which genres they are likely to attend to, but also as to what kinds of evidence is meaningful to them and how they would expect it to be gathered. Have you done the experiment or gathered the statistical evidence and done a cost-benefit analysis to argue to educational policy makers for the introduction of an education program? Have you had the appropriate spiritual experience and did you testify to it in a credible way to persuade a spiritual group that you understand their values? When you write about changes of media coverage of basketball, do you share in the excitement of the game?

If you cannot enter into the audience's world of objects and ways of knowing, how can you get them to turn attention to new evidence, attend to a different part of the world, and gather knowledge in a different way? Perhaps you can call on another role or identity that gets your audience to look in a different way, such as reminding the sports fans that they are also consumers in a very extensive market that is being manipulated by media corporations—and thus getting them to remember evidence and ways of knowing that are important to them in other times and places. Scientists are often directors of labs, and must attend to information and reasoning from the financial and legal domains.

Ontologies and epistemologies are not just philosophic abstractions; they are also practical matters of communication. To influence your audiences you need to know what they look at, what is important to them, and what they are likely to accept into their universe of attention. The more one enters into a field the more epistemology and ontology direct the reading and reception of audiences. Multidisciplinary or multi-group communications are likely to bring these issues to the fore, whether or not participants use philosophic terms to describe their differences of understanding.

INDEXING AND REPRESENTING OTHER TEXTS: INTERTEXTUALITY

Texts are not isolated communications. As considered in Chapter 4, they exist in relation to prior discussions in other texts, which create a world of facts of ideas which the readers are familiar with and which shape their knowledge, orientations, and concerns. To communicate with an audience you need to be aware of the texts that inform them. These texts can also serve as resources of shared ideas and information, topics of discussion, points of difference, or definitions of situations ripe for action. Behind and within the represented world is an intertext of similar and related texts which have previously represented that world and neighboring areas. The scientific report and the ethnographic account each is built on relevant literatures that have posed questions, brought a discussion to a certain point, produced related findings, identified appropriate methods, and set criteria for the current study to address. The current article must create a relation to this intertext and create a place for itself within a landscape it will change by its presence. Even the fairy tale rests on the memory and experienced pleasures of previous fairy tales.

The most explicit way texts rely on other texts is by quotation—a segment of another text is directly imported. Another author is allowed to speak for him or her self, to take over the voice the text for a moment. But of course the textual space is handed over to the other author with some cost—the gift is not a free will offering. The current author uses the words of the quoted author only for the quoter's own purposes, even if the purpose is to draw on the authority of the quoted author as an eloquent spokesperson for the quoter's cause. But the quoted may also be the drudge who has produced the facts and statistics that allows the quoter to weave fiery arguments, or the quoted may be the misguided holder of opinions to be the target of critique and derision.

This handing over the voice of the text is hardly a license for the quoted to say whatever he or she might desire. The quoter has control over which of the quoted words will be chosen—the quoter's only constraint is to transcribe the words accurately. The quoter also gets to introduce, discuss, and pass judgment on the words quoted. These words can be explicitly characterized as wrong, or silly, or misguided, or idealistic, or prescient. The judgment can be expressed subtly, with verb tense to indicate ideas of the past or present, ironies, juxtaposition with other quotations and statements, or placement in an unfolding logic—limited only by what the resources of language allow one to do. These characterizations bring us closer or make us more distant from the words we are getting filtered through the quoter's framing. While the quoted gets to speak, it is the quoter who gets to frame and construct the drama, and to tell us how engaged we ought to be in it, from what perspective we ought to view it. The constructed drama of multiple voices ultimately serves to set off the quoted's position, to carry off the writer's intentions and advance the writer's own voice: at the head of the parade he or she is marshaling, as the humble servant of past wisdom, as the encompassing spirit who can synthesize and embrace multitudes, or as the shining light that cuts through the veil of misguided foolishness.

Paraphrase and summary of the original writer's words provide even greater transformation of the original voice of the person cited. This allows the further subordination of the original voice to the purposes of the writer, either being homogenized into the writer's voice, spoken in the tones that sound like the voice, or further characterized and perhaps stigmatized as something other—perhaps as a target or a foil or as an ally from great distance. The gist, rather than the words, becomes imported and heightened as a social force within the unfolding narrative but without a sharp a picture of concrete other actor who asserts identity through his or her words.

As the distinctiveness of original words fade, it also becomes easier to detach their gists from any specific actor. Thus assertions can be subsumed into "opponents who claim . . ." or "common sense frequently tells us . . ." These hazy shadows can provide a context for the current circumstances while removing the author from direct confrontation with focused other social actors, identified and represented in their own words.

At its most subsumed but most common form, these socially received ideas and terms are simply taken as assumptions, a recognizable and recognized cultural and social landscape against which all new statements are made. Every discussion rests on the long history of discussions developing knowledge and terms and issues. Only sometimes, however, are readers reminded of long histories and commitments—"Freedom of speech, maintained only in the struggles of every generation, comes dearly—only by challenging the borders of the unspeakable in every generation can we fulfill the promise of growing enlightenment." At other times prior texts may be treated blandly, relying on common unthinking assent, so as to bypass serious thought or emotion, keeping attention only on a small bit of current news added—"Police officer Smith, about to stop a pick-up truck for speeding, noticed that the vehicle seemed to be operated by a dog sitting upright in the driver's seat." The typical text serves only as background to the variation that stands out for attention.

REPRESENTING THE MEANING OF THE INTERTEXT

Through deployment of texts and voices ranging from the specifically memorable to the background murmurs of "what everybody knows," writers are able to represent their chosen social context for their current utterance. By attention to, selection among, and strategic representation of these voices—bringing them forward or hiding them in the background, with shrill sharpness or honeyed sweetness—the author can orchestrate a relevant social reality.

Of course other voices that the reader might remember or have access to and consider relevant limit the writer's ability to create this social reality, for the reader can always evaluate the writer's proposed intertext: "Ahhh—the writer is just following the party line, citing the party hacks, and relying on tired old party reports." "Hasn't this guy read any history, doesn't he know . . . ?" "Why isn't she paying attention to the Biblical injunction against . . .?" The writer's representations of the prior intertexts and the positioning of the new statement in relation to the intertext must be credible and persuasive for the readers to accept the social reality, to accept the intertextual space the writer is creating, and then to consider the text as plausibly responding to the opportunities of that intertextual position.

Readers' memories or perceptions of relevant intertexts may be aided or hindered by the expectations of genre. Legal briefs are expected to be attentive to relevant law and precedent within the jurisdiction, and a judge may lose confidence in a brief that forgets the important case that every lawyer in the state ought to know. It is in fact a strategy of the opposing lawyers to remind the judge of all the other relevant law and precedent that make the case look entirely different. On the other hand, if the judge in reading the brief remembers some lines of poetry, those lines can at most serve as a stylistic flourish and not a germane fact or reason. Indeed poetic lines only rarely come to mind in the court as judges are much more likely to be preoccupied with the legal files in their brains and libraries as they read the brief. If indeed the brief writer wants to introduce the literary quote or a philosophic principle into a brief he or she needs to do some work to establish its relevance and to limit the amount of weight put on it. Its place is not self-evident and reliable within this genre within this activity system, and its presence is therefore unstable and potentially dangerous and destabilizing if given too much authority.

Similarly the genres of scientific articles in various fields suggest the literature that can and ought to be evoked, the standard and particulars of codified knowledge that need to be respected, and the usual degrees of play that individuals can use to construct a review of literature that paves the way for their new claim. Any person who wants to question the taken-as-accepted literature and codified knowledge, or bring to bear extra-disciplinary knowledge has rhetorical work to do to legitimate the construction of an unexpected intertext. In addition to defining the expected resources of relevant intertexts, genre expectations also constrain and direct the usual manners in which other voices are brought to bear—typical formulations, typical footnoting, typical evaluative phrases and characterizing moves. While a political commentator may be allowed to characterize a speaker as duplicitous, preface a quotation as evasive, and then display a brief quotation for its outrageousness, a political historian has to create distance more carefully and choose the quotations on different criteria. This is more than a matter of bluntness and politeness, or seeming objectivity. This is a matter of bringing the outside resource into the domain of a new discourse and having it serve as a useful and meaningful utterance in the new context.

DISCIPLINARY AND PROFESSIONAL LITERATURES

The regular explicit invocations of particular ranges of texts within particular kinds of articles identify professional literatures. These are the texts one is held accountable to knowing, drawing on, and placing one's current project in relation to. The texts that seem most salient for the current project are likely to be explicitly mentioned by the writer, particularly in an academic field with such practices, but it is fair game for readers to invoke any other of the texts that can be plausibly made to seem part of the relevant literatures—and the author is held liable then to address the difficulties or complexities arising from this invocation. On the other hand, texts from outside the professional literature of that domain can be generally assumed to be beyond the pale, leaving the writer free of responsibility for taking them into account.

The literature then comes to identify the knowledge within a field, and the work of academics can often be seen as contributing to a literature, expanding the boundaries of available statements for people interested in the kinds of things this specialty has to say. Thus in many scientific disciplines it is expected that in the introduction to research papers there is succinct statement of the prior relevant theory and research literature on which the current study relies and to which it seeks to contribute. If the article over time is accepted as reliable or true by other experts in the field and is used to help them carry forward new research, that helps confirm the interpretation of the literature in the article's review. Thus knowledge and the literature in a field gets codified (that is accepted and put in coherent relation) by an ongoing process of reuse, interpretation, and the emergence of a coherent story of what the many articles in the field add up to. Also freestanding reviews of literature, sometimes written by field leaders, bring together the literature of the field in a coherent way, adding up prior work and perhaps pointing to next stages of work needing to be done.

In these ways we can see each successful article, both new research contribution and literature review or commentary, as intervening in an ongoing discussion, both affecting the ongoing trajectory of the discussion and creating new landmarks which change the landscape which all future articles need to attend to. However, not all articles successfully enter into the professional landscape of the literature, or part of the expected chronotope that should be paid attention to in future articles. They may be seen as trivial, adding no new important insights or findings, or inaccurate, or just otherwise not worth attention. They may never get cited or used by anyone, and are thus forgotten in the collective memory.

We can extend this view of development of collective knowledge in academic writing to the deployment of intertexts in all writings. By attempting to create social worlds in which their statements best have meaning and thrive, in reflecting the perspective the writers wish to project, the intertextual assumptions of each article attempt to influence the reader's basic point of view, basic assumptions about the world, or what one could call the discursive construction of the world. Thus people may start to identify their changing beliefs about various aspects of life by the authors they are currently reading or the people they are listening to. They may even say, "I was so persuaded by reading a particular writer, that I started to read all her works and all the writers that elaborate a similar point of view." Even outside academic circles, where people do not talk in such self-conscious ways about their reading, the same phenomenon occurs, as readers are drawn into the world of sports biographies or model railroad hobbyist magazines by a particular text that introduces them to that world.

Intertextual fields then become domains of meaning established and maintained by social groups and that one enters into by reading, participating in them, and contributing to them. These intertextual fields serve as traditions of symbols that flow in and around the group whether or not these symbols are still attached to particular authors or particular texts. They become climates of opinion, ways of thinking, and ways of seeing and representing experience. These traditions of meaning themselves are bound up in the genres by which they are enacted. By entering into literate activity systems and participating in the genres, one enters into the rooms where these intertextual traditions are gathered and speak, where they resonate in every word. Just as Homer's epics resonate in the later day epics of Milton, Wordsworth and Kenneth Koch, and the common law resonates throughout contemporary court cases, yesterday's news resonates through today's papers and old office memos of a corporation still faintly chime behind today's email directive.

The terrains of intertext which new texts constantly re-invoke and cast in new light are an ever-growing resource, creating new positions to speak from. Writing in the twenty-first century is a far more complex and varied thing than it was five thousand years ago, or even one hundred years ago, in large part because of the expanding textual inventions and resources; the large numbers of text which one can echo, rely on, and set oneself against; and the complex social relations that have taken on institutional force through the sets of texts that define them. Thus, each new participant in recognizing that the law is the law, school is school, and Colgate-Palmolive is not RJR Nabisco, are also implicitly acknowledging the intertextual webs that support each and the way roles are intertwined with daily roles and relations.

CHAPTER 10

SPACES AND JOURNEYS FOR READERS: ORGANIZATION AND MOVEMENT

Texts are not just collections of information, though many texts indeed are primarily fact collections such as phone books and almanacs. But even these must be well-organized and make sense to the users. In phone books, organization is important for readers to access and make sense of the information they want readily. Almanacs with more kinds of information have varying organizing principles by topics, each of which has locally organized tables, lists, and similar information display devices, and there are chapters, tables of contents and indexes to help the reader find the appropriate display. The internet, digital searches, and hypermedia are changing display formats along with the principles of organization and access of informational reference documents, but still an intelligibly ordered structure is needed.

Encyclopedia entries have complex internal organizations beginning with the name of the topic, overviews, and a list of major topics (if there is an historical aspect that usually comes first), defined by headings, beneath which is a narrative paragraph or paragraphs presenting the information in a way that establishes the connection of the facts and making them easy to comprehend in the clearest language appropriate to the topic. There are also cross-references to other articles or related topics in the encyclopedia. The article usually ends with further resources. This organization is so useful for access and clarity that electronic media and hypertext have changed it little except turning the cross-references and other resources into links. The bigger changes have to do with multiple community authorship, which has led to the back pages in the wiki format, containing the history of changes, participants, discussion of issues and like material—all important for the management and evaluation of the collaborative contributions.

Texts that are primarily for the storage, quick access and retrieval of information have a predominantly spatial organization, so a reader can rapidly locate the spot with needed information. In writing such a text, one should keep in mind the readers' ease of location and rapid making sense of the desired information. But other texts, meant to be read sequentially (even if sometimes selectively) have more of a temporal organization, as reading occurs over time with readers introduced to one thing and the next. New forms of digital texts have both substantial spatial and temporal elements, as readers navigate spatially conceived hypertexts in temporally structured sequences, while also processing elements within each multimedia station or page. These digital texts present challenges for creating hybrid ways of thinking about how such texts can provide ordered, interpretable, meaningful experiences for readers. Here, however, I do not deal in detail with the rapidly changing developments in digital media, but rather present organizational and stylistic principles derived from traditional texts, even as they may now be produced and delivered digitally. Perhaps the comments provided here may be of use to consider the new hybrid spatio-temporal texts, but only time will tell what guidance will be useful in this moment of textual change. While I have some confidence that the more fundamental issues in the earlier chapters will be applicable in the digital world (though of course translated and freshly applied), I am less confident about how actual textual form will evolve under what principles, as these are so tied to the form and conditions of delivery.

Most traditional texts provide sequences of information, arranging them so they are meaningful as readers move down an information or reasoning path. The most obviously sequential text is a set of instructions which provides just the information the readers need to know at each point in accomplishing a task, and then gives the readers specific options based on individual needs or desires. The coherence in instructions comes from the sequential organization of attention to the objects and sets of actions. The meaningfulness and persuasiveness depends on the right things being presented at the right moments. If the reader-users cannot locate the dial to be adjusted at the right moment, or they do not understand the relation of two parts to be aligned, they may discard the instructions as not useful. At the very least they must solve some puzzles to be able to know how to move to the next step. Enough such difficulties may lead to a breakdown in meaning and distrust of the instructions. Further, if the results are not as anticipated or promised, if the recipe does not produce an appetizing dish, the reader is likely not to trust the source for future directions.

Directions must lead the reader down a clear path of action and produce acceptable consequences. The need is no less great when mental actions are at stake, whether intellectual or emotional. The readers must always know where they are and where they are headed. Even if uncertainty, puzzlement, or mystery are in fact an expected part of the journey, as in a mystery story or presentation of a philosophic quandary, the uncertainty must be specific and contained, limited to precisely those uncertainties that are expected and tolerated (if not in fact to be enjoyed) by the readers. Leading readers to cliffs and then pushing them off, loses readers—except for thrill-seekers, who are expecting such things from the kind of texts they choose. So an important part of the text is to create a tolerable, intelligible, and rewarding path, so the readers will understand where each step is taking them and will want to take the next step. Often this also means that readers need to be able to locate the relevant information in their memories to make sense of and understand what is presented, so that the text helps draw greater parts of their mind into alignment with the text, building richer and more forceful meanings as the text progresses. Reading is an effortful activity, where the readers have to work positively to give their minds over to imagining the writer's meaning. They can easily give up if the time and effort becomes too great, too unpleasurable, or too confusing—or if the text leads in directions readers do not care to go, that conflict with or are distant from what their minds already contain or think about. If because of external constraint, such as legal and financial consequences or school grades, a reader continues despite confusion, unpleasantness, or seemingly purposeless burdensome effort, the reader is likely to give only minimal and resentful cooperation. The readers are then like people on a forced march, hardly in the mood to appreciate the scenery or to give full attention to collaboratively solving the difficulties of the journey.

Organization of a text is about creating meaningful, rewarding, purposeful trips for readers through the information, narrative, argument, reasoning, calculation, and other material you want to present. The text needs to be presented coherently, so readers will be able to follow you in every step of the way with some engagement and enthusiasm, without feeling they are asked to take undue leaps of faith, to make excuses for you, to fill in gaps that you neglect, or to jump from one place to another with little guidance. And when the readers reach the endpoint you want to bring them to, they should feel the endpoint was worth the journey.

Thinking about organization as a coherent sequential journey through an information landscape provides a temporal perspective about reasoning, which is usually seen spatially as a consistent and supportable structure. Of course, readers, after they have read, may go back to examine the structure and overall meaning of the text, as we will consider later in this chapter. Even as they proceed temporally through a first reading they may be building a spatial model of the text's coherence, particularly if the text's conclusions are important for some work they need to carry out. Yet first, as they initially read it, they also need the experience of being carried along moment by moment, building meaning, maintaining comprehension and trust in the text, knowing where they are and not doubting any step they are being led down.

The following are some strategies for making the textual journey intelligible and trustworthy for the readers, but since genres vary so greatly in structure and activity, the following comments are framed very generally to be appropriate to a broad range of texts. Nor will these comments explain the many genre-specific details of language which are well covered in many textbooks, guidebooks, and other sources of advice, although it may point at well-known topics covered in these books, from which I have learned much and to which I have little fresh to add. Here I am just offering a fresh perspective for thinking about and using well known features of text and language. Similarly, I will not provide detailed examples, which are well covered in the many textbooks and guidebooks, in ways that are selective and focused for the kind of writing concerned. My examples here are only to show how wide-ranging the contexts might be where general principles could be applied. For any specific kind of writing, it is useful to consult an advice or stylebook appropriate to your task, genre, and audience. Further, in the long run, it is useful for any writer to develop practical familiarity with a wide repertoire of organizational and stylistic options, working with many kinds of texts. The wider the repertoire of style and organization, the greater choices the writer will have at hand at any moment and the better able the writer will be able to discriminate among options and choose the most appropriate to the immediate situation.

STARTING THE JOURNEY

Depending on the trust, authority and purposes of a text, readers may need more or less orientation to where they are heading, but in all cases the writer needs to engage readers' attention and motive to continue on the textual path. Even if you are relying on the importance of the subject to the reader, you still have to offer the promise of something new, interesting, or immediately relevant and valuable, even if only confirmation of beliefs at the moment when confirmation is needed. Beginning writers when given such advice about gaining attention may invent bizarre and barely relevant attention-getting devices. Even more mature writers may resort to well-worn devices like starting off with an evocative story to make personal an abstract or technical issue for a more general audience. However, one does not need to act like the barker at a carnival, saying anything to get the customer into the tent. A more sober approach is to identify what needs, interests, or concerns might have brought the readers to the text and then somehow speak to those motivating concerns. In some cases this might mean providing statistics about the magnitude of a problem and its consequences, while in other cases it might mean identifying a point at issue between two philosophers. Elsewhere it may be presenting the overview of the recommendations in a report that then directs people to the internal sections if they want to follow up on an issue. It all depends on the kind of document, the needs it serves, and the particular context it appears in. The strategies used in documents similar to those you will write can give you a sense of the collective wisdom of previous authors engaged in similar tasks. Recognizably evoking the motivations associated with a genre has the further advantage of helping the readers rapidly orient to the kind of text it is and the directions it will take. Thus the standard formats of scientific articles help readers locate the news or contribution of the articles, allowing them to decide which articles to follow up on and in what depth. Equally, business correspondence that is part of an ongoing negotiation or transaction often begins by identifying the specific case and previous relevant documents, with perhaps a brief refresher narrative of where the transaction stands.

TYING THE PIECES TOGETHER: COHESIVE DEVICES

Once you have the reader in the door you have to be careful about maintaining attention and good faith even if you must disagree, challenge, or otherwise irritate readers. It is easy for readers to be alienated and close the book and walk away. Or if they stay, they can become resistant critics, mentally constructing countertexts of alternative interpretations and evaluations. An important element in allowing readers to know where they are and how that relates to where they have been and where there are going is cohesive devices, that include

- Text markers, section identifiers, predictors of the reasoning or steps coming up, or summative passages tying together where one has been in previous sections, so as to launch the next stage.
- Transitional words and phrases that explain the connective logic between sentences or paragraphs, such as "therefore," "afterwards," or "as a consequence of."
- Compound and complex sentences that put several topics in relation. Even simple sentences can tie together multiple prior topics of discussion and launch new topics from previous ones.
- Pronouns that refer back to prior subjects, keep them alive, and provide continuity, but the reference must be clear. Texts soon wander into confusion if the reader no longer is sure which of many things an "it" can refer to.
- Precise use of verb tense to identify the time locations of specific actions and their relation to each other. The tense system is delicate and precise in most languages, but if used inaccurately can lead to as much

confusion as pronoun uncertainty. The common advice that one needs to stay in the same tense is oversimplified and inexact, but it does at least raise the issue of time confusion. However, even in the same sentences, some actions may be completed before others begin, and other actions continue while being punctuated by others, while still other actions may be in the future or be hypothetical possibilities. The delicacy of tenses in indicating complex time relations is shown by examples such as this: "After Samantha had completed her application form, she was waiting in the front office when an enraged young man ran out of the interview room muttering 'Never, never will this happen.' Samantha became apprehensive that her own interview would not go well and she would be leaving with a heavy heart."

- Repetition of exact words or core roots—what is known as lexical cohesion. Repetition of key terms allows the reader to keep track of main elements and plant them firmly in the imagination, following their progress through the changes of the text and arraying other elements around these key anchor terms.

- Using synonymous or related terms, to establish a limited domain of meanings and familiar relationships (or semantic domain), helping the reader make sense of the text. As one moves through a text, the semantic domains may shift following the logic of the organization and argument. Accordingly, the opening of an article on the economy might start in the daily business world of customers and shopkeepers with groceries, products, and prices, but as the discussion turns to underlying analyses the semantic domain might shift to that of economic theory, with supply and demand curves and equilibrium points. Nonetheless, for readers to understand how the argument fits together you will clearly need to connect one semantic domain to the next by some transitional move, such as "These daily actions are readily explained in theoretical terms . . ."

All these cohesive devices are related to and provide guidance for the reader about the underlying coherence of a text, but do not in themselves guarantee a sense of coherence for the reader. Ultimately coherence depends on the reader being able to build a picture of the text's meaning that fits together in a unified picture (even if that is intended as a fragmented picture of a fragmented reality, as in the portrayal of the chaos of a battlefield). We will examine this underlying issue of text coherence from the perspective of logical or reasoned arguments, from the perspective of emotions and stance, and from the perspective of the total picture being constructed. All of these have a temporal element, as the reader moves through the text, but all also have an after-the-reading residue, which can be viewed in a more spatial way.

COHERENCE IN THE REASONING AND REPRESENTATION

If the text is presenting a reasoned argument or examination of an issue or topic, the logical and evidentiary connection from one part to the next directs the readers down each step and gives them confidence that they move forward on solid ground, led by a trustworthy, reliable guide. Thus the reasoning that warrants each step of the journey should be made explicitly enough to reassure the audience that they are not taking faulty steps.

Of course at the end of the reading, readers always have the freedom to disagree and find fault, but in the course of reading they are granting their imagination to the author, even if they are holding some mental reservations because of disagreements or other questions. Each reservation they add distracts from the totality of mind they are giving over to the imaginative construction of your ideas and the personal commitment they are giving over to the meaning you are asking them to create. As these reservations or mental alarms add up, readers may begin feeling they are giving their minds over to an unreasonable person who makes unwarranted, unsupported, or bizarre claims, who is asking them to make unacceptable leaps. The natural reaction in that case is to say "I am not going to go there and I am not going to waste any more of my mental energy in this journey." If readers continue reading beyond this point, their interpretation of the text will be filtered through a negative characterization of the author or text, such as the writer being unreasonably partisan, just wrong, or comically foolish. Rather than constructing your meaning, the readers will be constructing a story about what is wrong with you and your text.

This also means there needs to be precision in what is said, so the reader knows what they are assenting to in their imaginative reconstruction of the meaning, and exactly how that provides a next step in the reasoning. Otherwise readers are likely to insert their own meanings, desires, or perhaps aversions into the underspecified story, leading them in a different direction than the path being set out in the text, with a consequence that the readers at some point may be confused, caught up short, or lost. Being sufficiently explicit in the text markers, transitional phrases, and other ligaments that tie the parts of the text together can help the readers to be precisely aware of how one step leads to another and to make the desired connections rather than following their own associations.

Although the above advice points in the direction of confident, directive statements, this needs to be qualified in a couple of ways. First, you should not be more confident, certain, or directive than you actually have the evidence and certitude for. This means you must be careful to qualify your remarks through modal verbs and hedging statements where appropriate, as well to recognize and address contrary points of view, especially if they are likely to come to your readers minds unprompted. Recognizing questions and alternative views may even increase the trust of readers, as they perceive you as an honest and reasonable evaluator of the evidence and logic. But this fairness then puts further responsibilities on the remainder of the text, to living within the limits that you have recognized, claiming no more than your argument has allowed, and keeping contained the questions raised by the concessions so that the readers can still continue down a path of reason, while carrying the uncertainties with them. If the counterclaims or evidence or uncertainties stop your argument dead in the tracks, readers may not travel much further with you. But carefully framing and limiting the concessions will allow you to carry forward, even though with lessened ambitions.

At the same time as recognizing and addressing legitimate difficulties, there is no reason to proliferate difficulties, doubts, or questions where these are not directly relevant to the direction of your argument. Nor is it usually necessary to include information and concerns not essential to the forward direction of your discussion issues if you are aware that they are likely to upset, confuse, or arouse opposition. That is, given the great variety of human perspectives and the delicacy of reading which can lead to readers' misunderstandings, multiple interpretations, loss of good will, and disruption of co-orientation, it is worthwhile considering what is necessary or useful to say, and what might serve to distract, divide, or lead astray.

Finally you also need to be aware of the sophistication of your audience. If you can be sure that many arguments, reasoned consequences, or information are familiar to the readers, you need not tell them at length what would be obvious to them. Tediously repeating the familiar will not respect their expertise, and perhaps even indicate that you do not understand what expertise in the field consists of—marking you as an outsider or novice with little authority to speak to the insiders.

THE SYNCHRONOUS SPATIAL PICTURE

While it is important to consider the steps in front of the readers and how you can carry readers forward on their journey, it is also useful to consider the accumulation of steps they have taken and how these fit together in laying out a picture up to any particular point they may have reached in the text. Your text gradually reveals a world of meanings to the readers. Although readers experience a journey through time, they also develop a more synchronic spatial or structural view of the meaning that at each moment has a certain shape and contents. This spatial construction of the meaning of the text may occur even if the reader does not read it sequentially, but probes it in different places, gaining pieces of information that add up to a picture of your text as a whole. For example, research scientists may skim the abstract at the front of the article then jump to the data charts to see the results and then jump to the end to see what the author is claiming on the basis of the data. If then the article is important to them or raises questions, they might jump back to the methods to see how the results were produced and then dig further into the results. Then some questions of interpretation might lead back to the theoretical section, and to the review of literature to see whether the authors were aware of related studies with other findings. But all this jumping around is not incoherent—it brings the readers into a deeper and more complete understanding of the text as a structured argument.

This synchronic spatial meaning is the kind that can be looked at all at once, perhaps represented in a summary, an outline, a flow chart, or a map. Such representations make simultaneously visible all the parts, relations, and sequences. This is the kind of representation a reader builds if he or she writes a summary or set of ordered notes on a reading, but a skilled reader can also build it mentally. A small child first learning to read may only be able to hold in mind a single letter or cluster being phonetically sounded out, or a phrase or sentence being made sense of, but as readers develop they are able to grasp larger units and see the smaller ones in relation to them to form a mental construct of the total text meaning. When readers have an adequate mental construction, encompassing the whole text, they say they understand it. Of course there are some texts that attempt to disrupt our constructing such a meaning or want to keep emphasis on the experience of a journey that constantly challenges our senses, but even such texts are open to post facto accounts. Even the disruption or destabilizing of meaning relies on certain senses built in each smaller sequence with disruption points of particular kinds at specific junctures; further, the cumulative experiences, moods, emotions, or transient states of mind are aggregated across the total textual experience.

This spatial sense is ultimately what we refer to as coherence, how the text as a whole holds together in our mind to form a lasting impression we take away as we move further from the text. After the fact of reading, we typically hold the text in our mind as a single event, having been completed, except for texts that provide extraordinary experiences of passage or where we read the text under remarkable conditions that lead us to recall the experience in transit. If a reader finds a text especially difficult, the reader my need to reread it, look over the abstract, review section headings, create an outline or other summative representation. Such activities rely on the meaning already built, but bring them to a further level of clarity and coherence, giving the sense of understanding the whole text with all the parts and relations.

Later in this chapter we will consider how texts end, punctuating the journey of reading, usually gathering it together, closing it off, and occasionally holding certain threads in suspensions or pointing forward to future developments—thereby further cementing the overall meaning of the text.

THE GRADUAL DEVELOPMENT OF THE SPATIAL MODEL OF MEANING

This spatial model of meaning does not usually dawn unexpected on the reader in a single moment. Rather it is built as the reader goes through the text, adding piece to piece and finding patterns of sense. Each further step can fill out this picture, make it larger, create a shift in perspective, overlay it with new colors or filters, or even establish counter images. But at each moment of reading the reader relies both on former knowledge and ideas he or she brought to the reading and all you have presented previously in the text out of which the readers construct what they believe your meaning or intent to be. The reading journey has led the reader into a world you have stage-managed, orchestrated, and articulated, particularly if the reader has trusted your representations at each step. The world you have constructed has inhabited the reader's mind, at least to the extent of giving some of his or her mind over to it, contingently. Each step into that world builds a bigger picture, and provides more reasons, more facts, more connections, more richness to believe it, to trust it, to see it as a viable world. Further, in coming to see the world you are presenting, each reader has used what he or she knows, thinks, and assumes as part of sensemaking, linking your vision to what the reader already has in mind, potentially reorganized around the representations and connections of your text. That is, the reader has thought the way you have asked the reader to think, at least contingently and temporarily. Mentally the reader will have walked at least once down the pathway you suggest, making it imaginable and leaving at least a mental trace. Even more, the world you have represented becomes context for interpreting each further sentence, paragraph, or chapter of your work to be read—that is, the reader has to continuingly exercise and strengthen the world you represent in order to understand the further parts of the text. Additionally, in imagining your thinking, the reader has imagined you as someone who makes sense, speaks to his or her mind, and sees things in ways that he or she can also see.

The implications for these processes of co-orientation, co-knowing, co-imagining, and co-thinking, are significant for how you construct your texts so as to maximize alignment, deep persuasiveness, and mental influence.

First, you must keep track of what you have shown the reader to each point: what elements, facts, objects, other texts you have brought into the text that evoke reader meanings, so that you can be aware of what exists in the world you are coming to share with the reader at each point in the reader's journey. Further, you need to keep track of the connections you make among these meaning elements and how they sit in relation to each other. This is exactly like the way a novelist must keep track of the characters she has placed in a novel, what she has said about each, what motives and actions drive each, what their interactions and relations are, how much they know and care about each other as to what issues there are between them as well as ongoing activities. The novelist must also be aware of the state of mind of each character so events and actions will make sense to the reader. What has been already presented must be factored into the ongoing momentum of each page of the novel, as new events and relations unfold based on all that is in place and in motion.

If your aim is expository or explanatory you need to make sure the reader sees and understands all the concepts and facts necessary at each point to understand what is going on and to be ready for the new element you will introduce. If your purpose is to set out a logical or evidential case, the reader needs to see what evidence is presented, what the reasoning steps are, what principles and arguments are established and how one builds on another. If you are presenting an inquiry process, the reader needs to see the concept and motives behind the inquiry and what knowledge and tools you (and the reader) have on embarking on the inquiry, then the plan for engaging the inquiry. When all the necessary information is on the table then readers may be able to follow your discussions and what you may conclude.

You may notice that each of these examples seems to follow the logics built into a number of well-known genres of exposition, argument, or research. Indeed, the historically evolved genres usually contain a kind of situational, task-based wisdom on steps that will not only lead a reader down a path, as well as for what readers need to know at each point to make sense of all that has been presented and to set the stage for the next part of the text.

Second, these elements must add up and make sense to the readers, so at each moment readers are engaged in a plausible imaginative universe. If the readers need to suspend judgment or accept confusion, or adopt some unconventional or odd assumptions that contradict common sense, you must give them warning, ready them for it, and have created enough trust so that they will temporarily suspend common sense to allow their imaginations to go to the place you direct. You must then keep this world of suspended judgment contained, so that having passed over the chasm of suspended judgment, the readers again find themselves on recognizably solid ground.

Third, you need to be aware of where and in what way you are evoking the readers' own experiences and perspectives. It is often useful to mobilize readers' own thinking and associations—after all as a writer you have only the imaginable meanings in readers' minds to work with, evoke, and shape through the prompts of your texts. But, unless your text is meant to be only open-endedly evocative, projective and associative—that is, you are happy to let the reader take the meaning anywhere they will following the only dynamics of mind and meaning released by the text—you need to keep those personal thoughts coordinated with where you are taking the reader, to keep them in the universe of meanings you want them to understand, connect with, and perhaps act on.

Fourth, every reader's journey is swathed in dispositions, orientations, and emotions that create a wholistic state of receptivity. Even rational arguments depend on evoking an appropriate state of mind in the reader so that they can absorb the reasoning—uninterrupted by outrage, comic distance, or melancholic longing for some preferable state of affairs. It is likely that underneath the argument there is a highly affective motive, whether a quest for truth, a desire to uncover manipulations by powerful figures, or the drive to find a vaccine for disease. Emotions and dispositions concentrate the mind and motivate readers and writers in their rational quests. Further, within the frame of such quests, particular findings or developments can be felt as exciting, disappointing, puzzling, frustrating, activating. So just because a text does not seek arguments based on emotions or attempt to evoke emotional states, nonetheless, states of mind and emotion are a necessary concomitant of all texts and tied to the writers' and readers' motivations. The more meaningful texts are for readers, the more deeply the texts mobilize the entire dynamic of their minds.

Some texts more directly engage the emotions—whether the evocation of certain emotions or states of minds are the ends in themselves, as in some aesthetic works, or they are a means of creating affiliation, opposition, agreement, approval, or other persuasive ends. These texts may represent emotionally evocative material in isolated moments, but the emotional trajectory of a text can be dynamic as events transform hope into disappointment, optimism into fear, fear into relief. In sequences of emotions, each state of being prepares or impedes the next, as well as provides the grounds for transformation. Some texts in fact are aimed at creating specific sequences of emotional transformation, such as an elegy that brings a reader from a devastating sense of loss through various emotions of grief to a final consolation and acceptance, or an advertisement that converts desires for excitement into desires for automobiles or anxieties about social acceptance into purchase decisions for hygiene products. In these one can follow the sequences of information, action and representation—of meanings—in relation to the emotional path being laid out for readers.

Rational or information-based arguments can also gain from attention to the sequential mental dynamics set in motion—as an identification of a problem may lead to an underlying analysis of the causes, an examination of the resources available for solution, a proposal, and an accounting of the costs and benefits leading to a recommendation. Each of these stages is associated with an orientation and state of mind of the reader along with specific contents. Discussion of a current political disagreement, for example, may lead to an examination of the underlying ideological issues and then a philosophic consideration of the vision of the world presupposed by each, followed by a consideration of the distinctive visions of the future of society. Each step in the text brings to bear different informational contents, forms of reasoning, and reader dispositions or states of mind, but each must persuasively grow out of the previous ones, translating the important motives from the earlier landscape into the new terrain, and the reader must be brought to the new step in thinking or state of mind. The new state of mind then reconfigures the interpretation, evaluation of, and stance toward the earlier synchronic space of meaning, perhaps even bringing out elements previously not attended to or changing the interpretation so radically as to transform the meaning of the earlier part.

LOOKING BACK

This dual consideration of spatial and temporal meaning of a text provides a more dynamic way of thinking about the conclusions of texts. Of course, some texts are just expositions of information and end abruptly, as when you reach the z's in a phonebook or fill out the last item in a form. Such texts do not ask readers to construct any challenging meanings or change their minds, other than to add a few informational items. But most texts require constructing a meaning or evoking sentiments, calling on existing information, mental relationships, and ways of perception and then integrating the new with the existent.

So if one thinks of the text as a taking readers on a journey into a set of meanings and through a set of experiences, at the end the readers should be able to view the material of that journey in a different or more complete way then at the beginning, and they also may be able to apply that new perspective to the world or thoughts outside the text. The end of a text is the last moment you as a writer have to help the reader integrate the meaning of the journey, understand the consequences and implications, reframe prior knowledge on the basis of the journey, translate contemplation into action, understand the text's value, and apply the text's meaning to some context beyond the text. Just as the opening engages readers from a world outside the text and organizes attention in a new direction, setting in motion the revelations of the text, the ending brings that journey to an end, adding it up and reintroducing the readers to the world, transformed by the meaning of the text which now resides in the readers' minds. The opening and closing sit at the borders of larger intellectual and practical worlds, and the textual journey has moved or transformed the reader into a new kind of agent, with new resources, perceptions, positions, thoughts, and information. Just as the introduction catches the reader into a world of meanings, the closing releases them outward.

One can think of the text as a time out from the rest of the world, when readers turn their minds to the contents and sequences the author displays for them to contemplate. This contemplation is a mental pageant holographically projected by the interaction of the text with the contents and pathways of the readers' minds. The closing can pull together that experience and provide some enduring impression that holds even when the experience of the complex journey fades and the time out is over.

CHAPTER 11
STYLE AND REVISION

In the end a text comes down to sequences of words on a page that carry the reader on a journey. The right choices of words add depth and engagement to the journey, while not standing in the way—by distracting, calling attention to themselves, or misdirecting the readers to think about things that vitiate the journey and meaning. Effective choice of words maintains and builds trust, brings readers to the mental and emotional space that makes them most receptive to the meaning, that does not irritate them or waste attention, that forms bonds of relation. There are many kinds of places you may want to take readers to, many forms of engagement, many relations, many meanings, many journeys—each with an appropriate style. Despite guidebooks that set out unwaverable rules for style, there are many styles. Style is a set of choices in pursuit of a reader's experience, and any single set of rules for style expunges the sources of style and resources that might be useful in some situations.

Style shines off the surface of a text. It may please the eye of the reader or glare harshly when seen in one light or another. Yet the sheen may have a depth that reveals the meanings, intents, and relations that are built into the text. Each of these levels—the surface, the social world of delivery, and the depth of meaning creation—can lend insight into what we mean by style and can point to how we can work on it. And each of these levels can inform the work of the others. I will examine these levels separately in an order perhaps opposite the way we are most familiar with them. Style is often recognized through surface figures in the text and the surface is something we think to work on in revision once our contents are set. Certainly, revision gives us the opportunity to heighten and refine the emerged style of the text, but style pasted on at the last moment with little understanding of where it comes from, where it goes, and what we want it to carry, can weaken and distract from the force of a text.

Of course in certain communities and actions, there are preferred, even mandatory, styles. Violation of preferred style can in itself irritate readers and even block communication. So in contemporary business communication, stylistic preferences for a direct, action-oriented, concrete style that stays within a limited vocabulary are so pronounced they can be dictated in handbooks of business style. Such handbooks exist for many domains, whether for a newspaper, for student assignments in literary studies, or research articles in psychology. In the academic world not only will the prescriptions differ among disciplines; they may subtly differ between those enforced on students and the practice of fully credentialed professionals.

Other kinds of more flexible resources are available on style. There have been training books throughout history giving neophytes practice in rhetorical and poetical figures (such as Puttenham's Arte of English Poesy, 1589). Other books recognize the variety of styles and techniques for modulating style to support principled choices among alternatives (for examples, Eastman, 1984; Lanham, 1978; Williams & Colomb, 2010). Additionally, functional grammars, which consider the functions of language underlying its forms, reveal general resources of language which can be deployed in varying circumstances. These can also be very useful if you put in the time to learn their specialized terminology, particularly Systemic Functional Linguistics (See Halliday & Matthiessen, 2004; or Stillar, 1998 for a simpler presentation). Rather than replicating the work of presenting the resources of style already done so admirably by others, I will be providing a way of thinking about style that can be applied in a variety of circumstances and in relation to a variety of perspectives.

EMERGED MEANINGS AND RELATIONS

As texts' motives, strategies, shapes, and meanings emerge through the writers' decisions as described in the last few chapters, texts develop ways of representing materials, defining relationships between writer and reader, and providing direction for each reader's journey and experience. As part of that process, specific wording arises somewhat spontaneously to fit these dynamics, constraints, and foci. I say "somewhat spontaneously" because style may not be foregrounded in the writer's earlier thinking, but still words are chosen to bring the meaning into communicable space. Writers always must be projecting words at the point of inscription on the page. As the constraints and motives of a text become defined, the writer may pause to consider what word or phrase will fit at this moment. Yet the word choice at this point is likely to be predominantly dictated by what the writer is trying to say and how the writer is trying to move the discussion along.

Nonetheless, earlier drafts and sketches contain a number of tentative commitments about how to represent the subject matter (whether in detail or summarily, highlighting certain aspects, selecting certain data indicators to represent a phenomenon, and so on) and how these representations might vary in different parts of the text. Similarly, reasoning, logic, or connections will be framed (whether allusively and by metaphor or by logical propositions, by producing experimental evidence or synthesizing prior work.) Further, writers in early drafts adopt certain stances and relationships with respect to the readers (whether as authority informing neophytes or inquirer making proposals to peers).

GENRE, DECORUM, REGISTER, AND ACTIVITY SYSTEMS

These early choices will likely have been guided by genre choices that imply perceptions of the situation, audiences, and activity systems—along with specific perceptions about the particular situation. For those familiar with the genre, genre choice will draw forth certain voice, personal stance, and relations to the reader. The experienced writer for a newspaper takes on the voice of the journalist or editorialist or financial analyst or sportswriter, depending on the kind of story. Decorum (speaking the right way for the situation) comes in some sense with the territory, if you are familiar with the territory. Failures to adopt the appropriate style, to choose the word with the right vernacular or technical ring, will strike readers as striking a discordant note, not quite in tune with what the text ought to be doing.

Described from a linguistic perspective, the range of appropriate choices can be characterized as register, but further specific choices arise from the specific situation, role, interaction and meaning being realized. In dramatic terms, in adopting a genre, the writer falls into character, able to respond with spontaneity, creativity and appropriateness to the specific scene. Most writing is part of continuing engagement in some ongoing social group and associated activities, and even in some ongoing project that is shared. Language is already floating around in the social context, identifying objects and ideas discussed, offering already made phrasing, cementing connections between ideas, establishing available evidence, and suggesting other texts that are relevant. In response to that environment of language and meanings the writer begins to coalesce a new set of meanings and intents, drawing on the linguistic and meaning resources at hand. Even when a writer has been working in privacy on a project over time—taking notes, gathering data, sketching out ideas, reading other books—there, too, terms already are floating around in the texts consulted long before writing the first draft begins. The emergent text crystallizes new meanings selecting from the language and representations already within the intertextual space.

For an insider, then, genre, decorum, register, and specific relevant representations are already at hand to use when the writer begins drafting. Genre, decorum, register, and wording are more problematic for the outsider or novice attempting to fit in within a discussion or communicative group they have not been previously been part of. Decorum manuals or style manuals are then typically for the novice, though some are used for regulation, to be referred to by the professional gatekeepers and decorum police, such as editors.

On the other hand, if some event radically changes the context, composition, and concerns of a group, the at-hand stabilities of genre, decorum, and wording may be disrupted, testing the inventiveness of all participants. The collapse of a long-standing governmental and ideological regime, for example, may shake up the discourses of politics and law, as well as of history, schooling, social sciences, businesses, and even family support services. Within the well-embedded, stabilized situation, however, genre, decorum, register, and wording only become major issues when the writer wants to bend, expand, or break the decorum—from the tactful inclusion of a fresh perspective to the intentional attention-grabbing transgression. The activity system with its genres and history provides tools of expression to guide behavior, even down to the level of word choice, phrasing, and use of appropriate graphic elements. With familiarity of genre, comes immersion in the language and way of representing, so expressions take on the form associated with the situation seemingly spontaneously.

REVISION FOR STYLE AND BEYOND

Viewing style as an outgrowth of genre-shaped emergent meanings provides a way of looking at revision as recognizing and heightening the expressive dimensions already taking shape in the earlier drafts. Revision, as well, can go beyond the local phrasal and sentence choices that cumulatively across the text may be said to constitute the style. Revision can look at fundamental issues of focus of the discussion, organization, selection and use of information and data, identification and presentation of intertextual contexts, or any other element that goes into the construction of the final text.

Revision is an ongoing process as we examine and reconsider what we have written. As we see what emerges, we can evaluate whether we like the direction it is taking or want to redirect it. As we commit to a direction and examine the results, we can consider how we can make the text more of the kind of thing we see it becoming—that is, how we can make the text stronger or more effective in terms of the text's emergent designs and objectives.

Sometimes this revision, a reflective look at what we are doing, comes in the course of producing the initial draft. Sometimes this revision occurs after we have a completed draft or a sketch to look at. Sometimes revision can send us backwards to do more drafting or even to find more information. Yet, revision more often drives us forward to take the text to where its design is telling us and to shed the unnecessary weight of extraneous diversions, doubts, and hesitancies in order to give the text presence, clarity, and force, as appropriate to the situation, genre, and decorum.

Feigning certainty where there is none and suppressing complications when they are relevant are usually not in the long run effective, for trust of the readers is the writer's most important asset. Nonetheless, advancing the statement with greatest warranted clarity and force helps the reader attend to the written words so as to reconstruct and align with the writer's intended meanings. The writer should seek to take the readers as far as possible into the meaning and intent while still maintaining their trust and cooperation.

DIFFICULTIES IN ADOPTING THE REVISION PERSPECTIVE

The trick of revision—that is, seeing a text freshly so as to be able to improve it—is to establish some perspective or criteria from which to view and evaluate components of the texts. It is not easy to get a fresh perspective or vantage point from which to read or evaluate one's text. We come out of the processes of writing having exhausted all our resources in coming up with the solution of what to put on the paper. We have done our best, and at first blush have no further ideas. Also mentally exhausted in the more usual sense of being tired, we have no desire to return into that space of hard work of meaning making to upset the fine network of solutions we have managed to piece together. That working state of mind was a transient mobilization of many cognitive resources; it is hard to reconstruct that state of mind, even if we know there are still some things to work on. Some people are so filled with anxiety about what they have written, they even have a physical aversion to rereading their drafts, let alone consider changing them. Eyes blur and minds numb when confronting the text, so one cannot even make sense of what one has written.

A focused set of concerns or criteria that directs us to ask specific questions about the text can give us positive, specific work we can reasonably accomplish and can help overcome resistance. The simplest questions to ask are those at the surface editing level. Are there any typos, spelling errors, or other transcription problems? We can examine the manuscript treating it as a spelling, grammar, and punctuation test. To do these tasks, all we need do is remember the rules we learned in the early school years and keep a dictionary at hand. Computer tools now can help us with this inspection by pointing out words or phrases that appear not to be correct for us to consider. Many experienced writers have these rules so internalized that often errors pop out spontaneously as they scan the surface of the text, and thus they may treat editing as a task just of rereading attuned to possible false notes. But professional copy-editors and proofreaders know that they need perceptual tricks to make the surface of the text visible, such as reading the sentences aloud or in the reverse order, or thinking of the sentences as grammatical structures rather than conveyors of meaning. And they need to keep reference books at hand.

Forms of surface editing point the way toward deeper revision in that they help create a distance between us and what we have put on the page. But deeper revision requires deeper questions, deeper tasks, and a greater separation from the words we have chosen to express our meanings. It is hard to read our texts to see whether they will make sense to readers who are not ourselves. After all, they made sense to us as we wrote them, and therefore looking at the text again may only evoke the meaning we already have in our head. Having another reader to point out lapses, confusions, or ambiguities helps us examine the text freshly as an expression of a set of coherent meanings. Even reading the text aloud to someone else may give us enough consciousness of the words to make us aware if we are making sense.

Learning to listen carefully to the criticisms and suggestions of others is itself a challenge. We may view their suggestions about language as either trivial or an attack on our meaning. We may view their failure to comprehend our ideas as an intellectual failure on their part. Or we may feel that their suggested revisions take the text away from our intentions. While we need not accept everything suggested to us, we do need to take every suggestion seriously to see whether it can improve the text. We need to be able to push the language to realize our meaning impulses even as we are ready to let go any particular formulations. We have to be ready to recognize that we make errors, that our initial choices can be reconsidered and improved on, that our ideas can become transformed as we find new ways of elaborating them. Such an attitude toward our own writing is only built slowly as we learn what perspectives other readers may have on our writing and we learn to give up our passionate attachment to our initial words as though they were parts of ourselves, while still remaining passionate about our impulse to communicate. Only once we have internalized that distant position of a reader, removing us from our texts to truly treat our texts as though they were fully outside of ourselves, then perhaps we can check the coherence of meaning by our own slow reading. When we can view the criticisms from others with some dispassionate judgment, we can begin to be dispassionate in judging our own writing.

DEFINING WHAT TO LOOK FOR IN REVISION

Making the text more of what it is emerging to be is challenging. For that we need to have a reflexive idea of what discursive space (or rhetorical situation) the text claims, how it is attempting to occupy and fulfill the potential of the discursive space, and a technical understanding of how it is attempting to do this. So we need to get outside of the text we have cobbled together in the heat of struggle. We need specific things to look at and criteria to evaluate the text by, for otherwise we will either see little or we will circle around our own self-doubts, with no guarantee any change is really an improvement rather than just a digressive response to uncertainty.

It helps to define different parameters of the text that we might reconsider. At the style level we have been considering in this chapter (as well as at the other levels examined in previous chapters) we can consider the interpersonal dynamics the text is setting up and whether we are satisfied with them, whether the text projects us in roles we are comfortable with, whether we occupy too much or too little a presence, whether we are inviting and respectful enough with our readers, whether the text provides adequate roles for them and accommodates their likely varieties of views and knowledge. Similarly, we can look at whether our ideas are present cohesively and the directions of the arguments and ligaments of the text are marked well enough to provide guidance to the readers as they attempt to find the inner coherence identified by the outward markers of cohesion. Further, we can look at the specific ideas and information presented to see whether they are identified adequately, whether all relevant parts are presented, and whether reasoning processes are made visible.

Similarly, revision provides the opportunity to consider the implications of the genre position we have taken. How consistent is the text in pursuing the aims inherent in the genre? If we adopt hybrid genres, is the combination effective and do the readers have enough clues to understand and accept what the hybridity is attempting to accomplish? How might the generic features be heightened, toned down, or played against each other to sharpen the message, emotion, or presence? How can we strengthen credibility in the projection of ethos or maintain the most appropriate stances for readers? How much passion of what sort, how much reason, how much of an associated mood, are appropriate to expand thinking, build confidence, or allow the reader's thoughts grow in appropriate directions? How much precision and univocality of meaning is needed given the nature of the genre and the task?

One way to identify issues to pursue in revision is to articulate through discussion with others or through extended written comments to ourselves a description of what we have produced and what we hope to accomplish. This then can provide us with a series of questions by which to interrogate the draft in terms appropriate to the goals of the final text, realized at every detail of language and composition.

Although the process for adopting a systematic stance toward revision which I am presenting here seems to be ignoring the spontaneous sense that there is something wrong or not yet fully realized, I am suggesting rather that any such intimation, intuition or unease is best elaborated so that we know what is creating the concern. This then can be turned into a systematic principle or query stance that can then guide revision. Since in producing emergent phenomena we don't always know where we are going—we are just following what seems good to us—only as issues emerge can we start to articulate them. This is particularly so if we are in a flow state where we are drawing on all our resources doing complex problem solving in real time, at the limits of our working memory and drawing simultaneously on less conscious forms of calculation and emotionally signaled estimates of success, as discussed in the next chapter. It is important not to interrupt that flow state or interpose too many forms of conscious monitoring in the moment. Yet after an hour, or a day, or a month, after being able to look back on the text, then we can start to articulate what it is that has emerged. Then we can begin to sense where our lights were leading us and identify means to take us more effectively to that place.

REVISION AND THE PROFESSIONAL STANCE TOWARD WRITING

Another way to think of this revision stance is as a professional view of writing. Professionals in any domain constantly work on their craft and monitor what they do to improve performance. Musicians, though driven by a love of music, practice their technique, do exercises, listen to tapes of their performances, and play before coaches and instructors to find out where they need improvement. Then they do appropriate exercises and self-consciously monitor their performances to ensure they are incorporating the new skills and avoiding bad habits. This professional attitude does not diminish their love of the music; it only increases their expressive potential through finer control of the directions and details, and gives them even more reason to love their art.

Professional athletes, likewise, no matter how much they love their games and feel they have great talent, do exercises, get critiques from their coaches, work on particular skills, and monitor themselves with awareness of those things they are working on. They are aware that performance is different than desire or impulse, though these internal feelings may lie behind their performance. The performance, nonetheless, must be realized through detailed, skilled, practiced behavior, responsive to informed criticism. Of course, professionals can sort out the difference between useful advice and uninformed suggestions from those who do not understand the craft, but they know the value of accepting any criticism, no matter how painful, that helps them recognize an area of weakness that could use work. This does not decrease commitment to sport, skill, and accomplishment of performance. Rather the commitment to craft only increases commitment to the game and a realistic sense of what goes into an accomplished performance.

In writing we are very attached to our words by our impulse to communicate and to the meanings that well up from inside ourselves to reach out to others. Further, the technical skills of text manipulation seem so complex at the same time as being so closely tied to meaning, that it is especially hard to view the performance as something to be worked on. We may even feel the attempt to revise as an intolerable burden that somehow interferes with our meaning and impulses. Yet revision gives us opportunity to see our text from the outside and improve it to realize our impulses more forcefully. We can look at our sketches and drafts, and keep working on them in semi-privacy before we send the final polished version to the intended audience. This allows us to become more objective in seeing the texts as symbolic objects, constructed and to be improved, rather than as direct overflows of our subjective states and excited thoughts. In the end we will have greater expressive potential, greater success in communicating our meanings and more influence on others, even if the revision process at times seems cold and technical.

CHAPTER 12

MANAGING WRITING PROCESSES AND THE EMERGENT TEXT

The guidance in this book has focused on the identification and crystallization of the communicative space—the textual version of the rhetorical situation—and the emergence of the text in that space. The focus has been on the textual object being made, the actions it is carrying out, and the people it is going to. Although the ultimate product is external to the writer in the form of a text that travels in the world, much of the work and meaning that makes it happen arises from within the writer. When the task is familiar and simple we may not think much about our writing processes, as the writing solutions may be immediately at hand. A memo similar to many we have seen and have written many times may be more an exercise in typing from memory with a few local adjustments than difficult problem solving. But as the difficulty of the task increases, it helps us to be able to understand our processes, manage them to best effect, and adjust them to fit the particulars of the task.

The previous chapters have discussed how to conceive of and direct the work to make that emergent document as though the writer were fully rational—but humans aren't built like that. Even our rational, conscious, and self-aware processes work in curious ways. These psychological complexities have their origin in the complexities of neurobiological human nature; the richness of our experiences; the limitations of our attention; our self-perceptions of identity, roles, and relationships, and the potential (or imagined) social consequences of our words.

This volume, particularly in the last few chapters, has focused on a writer working individually in semi-privacy, though with input and response from others. This chapter continues in that vein. Much writing in organizations and disciplines, however, is accomplished collaboratively, with work negotiated and distributed among many participants, and managing that collaboration requires particular skills and organization of the tasks. Nonetheless, all the tasks and functions presented here can be reconsidered in a collaborative context. Even some of the personal issues of anxiety and risk discussed later in this chapter, are often played out in a collaborative context, but with the advantageous potential of these problems in some team members being recognized by others and brought to explicit discussion and management.

In this chapter I want to give an overview of some of the many psychological issues that may play out at various moments in this emergent process, starting with when we enter into a situation that may call for writing.

IDENTIFYING AND WORKING WITH WRITING EPISODES

As discussed in Chapter 3, the impulse to write arises in response to situations, so writing begins with recognition of a rhetorical situation where we see people and events around us coming together in an exigence that we feel can be influenced, affected, or constrained by our words. The recognition of people, events, exigence, impulse, and possibility of influence all involve individual perceptions, and judgments. The accuracy of those perceptions and judgments are likely to affect the success of our endeavors.

Sometimes it is easy to perceive with some accuracy our need to respond the people and events outside us, and even the likelihood of our influencing events through writing. If students are enrolled in an academic course, and the instructor announces an assignment of an essay that must be completed in class that day to count for 10% of the course grade, the students are immediately mobilized to read the assignment prompt and begin thinking about it. Unless unprepared or confused, the students will soon be writing and focused on the task. If it is, however, announced that the assignment will be due weeks later at the end of the term, only some of the students are likely to feel an immediate need to start thinking about the assignment, gathering the materials, and interpreting the instruction of the course through the need to produce the paper, while others may not start feeling any exigency until the night before the due date. The ones who perceive the exigency early can devote more work and attention to the task through a more extended process, and are likely to do better. In such an example, we see the value in recognizing and committing to a rhetorical situation early when we find ourselves in it. The more clearly and immediately we see it and commit to it, the more we can gather and interpret information, think about our purposes and focus, and allow our response to emerge over time with multiple levels of thought and work.

There are many instances where we are handed assignments by others, whether on the job, from government, or in the community. We are asked to write a report, file a document, or prepare publicity for neighborhood fair. We are in effect told what the situation and events are, who the relevant people are, what is at stake, and our ability to affect the situation (if only to avoid the penalties of not doing what is requested).

At other times, however, it is up to us to recognize how events and people come together to create a situation calling for our writing. No one but ourselves perceives it is time to write a personal letter, submit an application for a job, or begin a book, although we may perceive external pressures that push us to those actions. The extreme case of self-defined writing episodes is personal reflective writing, impelled only by inner compulsion to sort out emotions, events, and thoughts. Our decision to open a notebook depends entirely on our perception of our needs in our current situation, but making that choice then establishes a commitment to a writing task and initiates a writing episode.

DEVELOPING AND MAINTAINING THE WRITING ORIENTATION

The very impulse to write is based on a kind of psychological orientation to action, arising from our perception of the situation. This is what psychologists call arousal. Something has caught our attention as potentially needing some action, so we attend, gather information and start weighing choices of action, whether conscious or not. Recognition of this state of focused attention directed toward action is worth noting, so as not to deny it or fight against it, but rather to make most of it. In a state of arousal, brain systems are mobilized and neurological chemicals are released, heart rate and blood pressure go up, and senses are more alert and ready to act.

A century old principle of psychology (the Yerkes-Dodson law) correlates arousal with quality of performance, but if arousal is too great, performances may suffer. This suggests for writing that recognition and self-regulation of one's level of engagement in a piece of writing may help keep one at the maximum level of performance—working hard but not overwhelmed. Many writers have experienced the pleasure and focus of writing episodes, where all one's attention and energies are focused toward the object of creating a text, but many have also experienced becoming so obsessed or so stressed that they no longer can think straight. At the extreme they no longer can decide what to do next or what words to put down: they are exhausted with a welter of conflicting ideas, and they suffer tunnel vision and decreased memory. They can no longer solve problems and are caught in an impasse. When writers reach that point then they have to turn attention away from the writing task and do something else until they can think straight and separate useful ideas from noise.

Awareness of one's state of arousal can help the writer see and accept the need for an extended, punctuated writing process that allows for regular periods of work, interspersed with breaks and engagement with other tasks. This is part of the core wisdom behind recommendations that it is better to write for short, regular periods every day rather than for extended concentrated sessions over a short period of time. Multiple moments of attention over many different sessions also allow the writer to focus on a limited number of things at a time, but gradually covering all the multiple levels and focuses of attention the complex document may need. In addition, awareness of arousal can also alert writers to the difficulties that might come with narrowed attention. Reviewing drafts after placing them aside for days or weeks allows one to reexamine the writing when one's mind is no longer encased within tunnel vision.

Being in an aroused state of writing is a bit different than arousal in a brief sexual episode, or in a fire, where one is intensely focused for minutes with all else fading from view. With writing, this period of engagement with a text may extend over days, months or years, while other aspects of life continue. Unless the writing task is short, one cannot give undivided attention to the writing task from start to finish. Learning how to regulate the intermittent periods of full attention, knowing when is enough for each day, each session, also means the writer needs to learn to keep the task alive in a more subdued mode during the interim periods. Without constant commitment and regular return to fuller attention, the mental orientation to the project may evaporate. The writer can readily lose a sense of the emergent impulse and emergent text, as attention turns elsewhere. Even if the writer maintains a commitment to a project, if he or she cannot find a way to bring attention back into the project and recreate a state of mind where the writing project dynamically grows, the project can fade from attention and commitment.

The writer needs to build skills to return to the mental place of writing where a perception of the task and situation has formed an impulse to communicate and is crystallizing in a set of meanings and textual forms. Letting the mind refocus and reassemble its internal attention and resources toward written action is a form of meditation and mental composure. Beginning writers may only be able to visit such a writing state of mind in the presence of supportive mentors, and each writing session is a fresh start. We can see this in young children whose ideas for writing are prompted by questions from adults who remain in the vicinity to help with problems of formulation and transcription so the child can remain on task. Even at university level, facilitation by an instructor or tutor at crucial junctures helps students focus on a writing task and overcome difficulties that might lead to loss of direction and vitiation of attention. Even very advanced writers may have difficulties mentally recovering projects that have been long dormant or challenging projects that strain their mental resources. Nonetheless, practiced writers over time can build their ability to remember the motives and processes of an emergent text, where they were in the text, or even more pertinently in their mind—over a day, a week, or even months.

This process of re-calling the writing project to mind can be helped by, at the end of each writing session, leaving off at a place where it is easy to restart, rather than at a place of impasse. This requires recognizing that you are approaching the limit for the day and stopping at an opportune place before reaching that limit. Perhaps sketching a few sentences or phrases indicating the way forward or outlining the next section and identifying topics to be covered can help remind you where you are headed. If you are not quite sure where you are heading, briefly writing out the problem that needs to be solved before you go forward can at least remind you what you were working on, and may even give you something to mull over before the next writing session. If you foresee an extended period where you will not have the focused time to do the deepest composition, may set yourself some lower order tasks that you can take on as discrete units. For example, if I foresee as the summer ends that I will have only limited time and attention in the coming term, I might identify some material that needs describing, or some sections needing polishing. I will then set up those tasks so I know what I have to do with the limited time, attention, and energy available to me in the next few months. This way I can keep making progress without having to bring the whole project to mind and without having to occupy my whole mind and state of being in the project while I am also occupied with other compelling tasks.

When I come back to the text, I have tricks to pick up the breadcrumb trail. I draw on all the relaxation and focusing techniques I have learned from performance arts, sports, and meditation practices to remove extraneous thoughts and focus on the work at hand. I work at places conducive for concentration, depending on my mood, whether it is at my desk with a cup of coffee or in a quiet corner in a coffee shop if I feel I need others around me (though not disturbing me) to help me concentrate. If I am still mentally not there, I begin revising earlier sections, creating outlines of the most recent sections I have written, or free-writing about my current thinking. If the project has been dormant for a while, I may work my way back into the text by looking over some of the source texts or theory, reexamining data collections, or reading. At times I may even impose on someone else as I talk aloud my thoughts on where I have been and where I am heading. These actions may take minutes, or days, or even longer to reprise extended projects that have slid into the further recesses of my mind.

This slow cooking of projects over time has added benefits and dangers. It provides time to solve numerous puzzles, take in more information consciously and unconsciously, and play around with many solutions, configurations, and strategies. While we may not be aware of the relevance of some of the stray thoughts or observations during these fallow periods, they may indeed be part of drawing on resources and ideas from surprising sources to help find ways to solve problems. We are relieved of the tunnel vision of intense concentration and can explore more widely. Yet all of this requires that the project remain at least activated at some level, with commitment and attention somewhere in the back of the mind. Awareness of a project on slow simmer, on the other hand, may raise anxiety about an incomplete project with many things left to be done, but as we gain confidence that cooking continues even at a slow rate, we become more comfortable with the project evolving at its own pace. In slow cooking, however, one must keep an eye on the pot so as to adjust it to the right temperature. A very slow cook that still leaves one with almost all the work to do at the last minute may be little better than starting the night before. This monitoring of the pace of the project is also part of the work of successful writing.

Just as an individual enters a state of arousal when beginning a writing episode, a group of people or an organization is mobilized for a period as they recognize and commit to writing tasks. While there may be focused moments of intense group collaboration and attention in developing plans or forming core texts, there may be other moments of individuals and the group attending to other tasks. While individuals gradually make their own progress on their separate contributions, the group can periodically return to discussion and planning to reestablish coalignment or one person may coordinate the work and monitor the overall progress and meaning of the document. An organization can work on an even slower time scale, setting in motion information-gathering and analytic processes, to eventually lead to a report or a plan or a sales documents years down the line. While there may not be frenetic group activity and other aspects of the group life may get more attention (at least until the latter stages of producing the final document), yet there is a continuing group activation moving the project along. If that activation vitiates, progress on the document fades.

RESISTANCES TO WRITING

Recognizing that we are entering into a writing episode creates challenges, challenges that we may prefer not to have. First, a writing episode requires cognitive work, sometimes quite strenuous, exhausting, and even painful and debilitating work. Writing is hard work that can produce headaches along with all the ultimate pleasures of accomplishment and discovery. Second, this work requires a commitment that puts an obligation on us and becomes a statement of what we value to others. Third, writing defines a relationship to others, represented in the text or to whom the text is addressed, and we may not feel fully comfortable with the commitment, confrontation, criticism, affiliation, or other social positioning that is emerging through the text. Finally, commitment to acting in a situation puts at risk—of both failure and success and the consequences of each.

Often enough ignoring work assignments or public debates over rezoning our neighborhood may require less effort and evoke less anxiety. One common method of avoiding recognizing we are in a potential situation is to believe we have little influence over events, and that our statements would be unlikely to change any outcomes. In this way we erase the possibility of a rhetorical situation and we don't even begin to search for kinds of genres that might have an impact or the kinds of things we might have to say. We just do not take on the commitments and obligations, work, and risks of the situation. Another common method is to put off thinking about the situation until the last minute when we do the task in a rushed panic that does not allow us to confront the full complexity, meaning, and potential of the task. Or if we procrastinate really successfully, the time will pass and it will be too late, relieving us of all obligation, even if we have to live with the consequences of inaction.

Once we have recognized there is a situation and made a commitment—perhaps because we want to keep our job or pass a course, or more positively because we anticipate enjoyment or success—then we still have many ways to resist, slow down, deviate, or wander from the task. Internal criticism about our ability to produce may keep us from setting to work with a whole mind, and cause us to question our choices at every stage from first definition of the situation to every grammatical choice. This questioning from lack of self-efficacy is far beyond the reasonable monitoring we need in order to evaluate our choices and consider alternatives. This self-questioning in particular may be fueled by our doubts of how our words will appear to others and how they will evaluate those words. When we put words on paper we are making a statement and committing to a public presence that may endure. This anxiety about our presence may go well beyond our spelling or grammar, which others may use to stigmatize our education and intelligence, to the opinions, perspectives, knowledge and reasoning we inscribe for others to look at carefully over time. People might declare us as right or wrong, informed or ill-informed, interested in trivial topics or important ones, too political or not political enough, advocating the right side or the wrong side. By writing we commit ourselves to roles, whether as an applicant for a job or as a poet or a reporter for a hobbyist newsletter. The anxieties raised by such concerns may lead us to wander from the task or may cloud our mind so we cannot think as sharply as we might, or to veer away from the topic and most anxiety-provoking or challenging issues as we write.

Robert Boice in his very practical book *Professors as Writers* (1990, useful also for non-academics) summarizes the extensive literature on psychological resistances to writing and finds the following diagnostic behaviors for people with blocking problems: work apprehension and low energy when writing, dysphoria, evaluation anxiety, perfectionism, procrastination, and impatience. These he finds related to the following causal factors: internal censors or critics, fears of failure, negative early experiences, general state of mental health, personality types, work habits and attitudes. He offers many useful ideas for short term and long term ways of improving productivity and overcoming these resistances and their causes.

PROMPTING AND ACCEPTING THE MUSE

Writers sometimes have golden moments when the writing overtakes them, and they feel compelled to sit down and transcribe the words flowing through their heads. They awake in the middle of the night or pick up a notebook in the middle of a journey, then lose all track of time as they seem to be transcribing words handed to them by the muse. Such moments have been reported sufficiently often for them to become iconic for the experience of "really writing," and some people will not sit down to write unless they sense such an inspired moment to be overtaking them.

But for such a moment to arise, the writer's mind must already be working on a writing problem or another problem that finds its expression in writing, whether the writer has been consciously focused on it or not. A writer who recognizes and is committed to a writing episode and is consciously working on the problems posed by the writing is more likely to assemble pieces that will come together in such moments of deep flow, as Csikszentmihalyi (1975) has described the experience. As writers, we gain if we learn to take ourselves regularly into places of complex problem solving, no matter what fears, pain, risks, or tempting distractions may stand at the entryway—even when inspiration hasn't quite taken over. Regular work, a short set amount every day, even if uninspired is more likely to define the problem you are working on, identify resources, consider possibilities, and otherwise set the table for when the muse decides to arrive (or more accurately, when your mind finds a set of solutions that is generative for producing text).

The impulse to write within one is more likely to blossom if you make space for it and invite it. Having set the table with the preliminary work, you still need to commence the meal—creating moments to confront all that you have assembled, to listen to the inner impulses bringing the disparate pieces of the task together, and to attempt solutions. Setting moments to examine the pieces you are working with, seeing how they are fitting together, and shaking them around will increase the chances that they will fall in place and a clear direction forward will emerge.

The muse, or the creative problem-solving thoughts, moreover, when they arise, may not always be pleasant—for such reasons as discussed previously of anxiety, overtaxing one's brain which may become oxygen depleted, and challenging settled mental organization. We may then experience exhaustion accompanied by dysphoric feelings. Words pressing to be expressed can feel raw and pressured as they emerge. This is all the more reason why we need to commit to regular work and regular times, so we confront this difficult and sometimes painful work. At times I have felt I need metaphorically to chain myself to my desk. Writers often need to find a quiet room far from distractions, and not emerge until they have gotten past the hard parts. Some go out of town and rent hotel rooms. Numerous rural writers' colonies are organized so there is little to do but write.

This commitment to confront the taskmaster muse does not mean we should torture ourselves when we reach an impasse. When the mountain is too high to climb at the moment, we can select a smaller preparatory task, head off in a related side direction for a bit, do some warm-up activity like free-writing or sketching out goals. We may even on occasion walk away for a bit, having looked the task in the face for a time and finding no way forward. While we turn to other tasks our mind can continue to sort out what the problems we have framed. But then we need to re-gather our thoughts and courage to return to the task. Otherwise, the mountain remains unclimbed and the text never written. But then also come the wonderful moments of parts falling in place, discovering new ideas, surprising phrases appearing on the page, and satisfaction with accomplishment. The climb is strenuous and muscles may be sore, but the mountain has its pleasures and rewards.

TRUSTING THE PROCESS

We have to accomplish many kinds of work in writing—and except for simple and familiar tasks all this work rarely happens in a single piece, despite our hopes that it will all come in a vision, as symphonies purportedly came to

Mozart—with all the rest just being transcription. Such visions in themselves indicate the mind has already been working on a problem, whether consciously or unconsciously, and there is one fortunate, memorable, glorious moment when all falls together. Further, even if we are fortunate enough to have had a vision of the overall structure and gist of a text (this does happen), yet there are still many details and levels of work that need to be pursued to bring the text to realization. I remember visiting an archive when over the course of a few hours the vision of what was to be the book *The Languages of Edison's Light* (Bazerman, 1999) came to me, but I had been working on the rhetoric of science for over a decade, and I had specifically been working on electricity for three years, with several papers already written. And then it took another ten years to carry out the detailed research, write and revise the chapters, and work with the publishers to bring the book to press.

So writing is inevitably a process, even if it is just in two-minutes for reading an email, recognizing we need to respond, deciding what we need to communicate, framing the best words, and proofreading before pressing the send button. Whether the process lasts two minutes or a decade, the initial impulses and words on the page may not be anywhere near what the final completed document will be. The imperfection of the first words may lead to despair at the limits of our accomplishment and the immensity of distance we still have to go, but awareness that there is a process to guide us can give us confidence and direction, limiting our work and attention at each moment with the assurance that we will be able to attend to other matters at some point in the future. It is a relief to not feel we have to solve all problems simultaneously and keep everything in mind all at once; we are then able to focus our inevitably limited mental resources on one item at a time.

Process is not a fixed sequence, as it is sometimes taught in school, because each task, each set of conditions, and each personality working with particular sets of resources calls for different ways of working and different sequences of events and attention. The standard processes taught in school arise out of the particular conditions of assignments set in the classroom to be completed in a relatively short time, with resources largely already in the student's mind. Although such a model that moves from idea-generation through drafting to revision does not fully recognize individual differences, it does serve well enough to introduce students to the idea of process. But outside school some tasks must be done in two minutes and others may continue for years with no fixed deadline; some tasks require great attention to social politeness while others require extensive reading or fact gathering; some are parts of large collaborative projects during the work day and others are personal projects done in spare time; some are strictly regulated in bureaucratic coordination while others are improvisatory or even disrupted by untimely addition of constraints or new information. Processes necessarily vary to fit the tasks. Moreover, especially as tasks become more complex, people have different preferences about how the work should be done. Yet there is always a process.

Explicitly identifying and understanding the process you are engaged in will most directly help you identify what you are primarily working on at each moment and what is the next task in front of you. It will also make possible an overview to make sure that all the necessary work will be done and all the dimensions of the task will be addressed. Most of all, it will relieve you of the debilitating sense that everything must be worked on at once and the equally debilitating sense that the text has not gone far and is riddled with problems. There will be time to go further and to address each problem in its time. By seeing that there is a process, you can come to trust the process.

Of course the mind is unruly and the emergent text is constantly suggestive of what needs further to be done. So you need not be a slave to your initial process plan and you can adjust it—whether doing new research to cover a new essential topic you uncovered in writing, adding in new rounds of discussion with the management team to identify their goals more clearly, or suggesting an alternate strategy that occurred to you as you put the facts together As you read a draft, you may realize you need to rearrange the order of your paragraphs, or you need to change the tone of the sentences. Equally, if in sketching out early ideas you get an idea for a way of phrasing a crucial section, you may want to spend some time in carefully drafting a short section before returning to the sketching ideas. Although you may be far from proofreading, if you see a few misspellings and typos you might want to fix them, but you don't have to, either, because you know you will get to that later—it is just easier and more convenient to do it now, as long as it does not distract you from the task at hand. It would, however, be a waste of time to correct every spelling and typo in a draft so rough it is possible you may not use much of the exact phrasing you have at the moment.

Trusting the process is particularly important in the earliest stages of writing when ideas about what the final text might look like may be unformed and uncertain, with little concrete direction. At this moment, we may be casting widely outward to understand the situation and discover what might be useful resources, while looking inward to discover our interests and concerns in the situation and what we want to say. Such work requires some presence of mind and freedom from anxiety. Yet this may be a place of great uncertainty, needing the greatest courage and confidence to face—the hardest place to step up to the task. We need to have great trust in the process to begin and give our work directions that will become more focused as we progress.

LIVING WITH OUR LIMITATIONS
WHILE DEMANDING THE BEST

As our text emerges, almost inevitably we will find flaws and limitations. As our unformed impulses take shape in words they may seem less grand and transformative, less novel and creative than we first thought. What seems large in the struggles of our mind, turns into something smaller and specific in the world. As we draw on the language and resources we find around us, the received language and knowledge of our society, our words can start seeming more similar to others, and perhaps less impressive. Psychologists may talk of confronting the grandiosity of narcissism, but we can also recognize that the world of communication is concrete and specific using genres, language, and situations already richly formed in prior interaction. Each utterance we add only moves the discussion and interaction along, sometimes with more force and redirection than other times, but rarely in the transformative way we imagine. Communication brings us from our private world of mental changes to the complex of social interactions. The more people involved in those interactions, the more our words will have to intersect with the thoughts, beliefs, forms, and words that move others. Moving the minds of many requires entering into familiar shared worlds of meanings.

Further, texts in process are unfinished and will rarely be as impressive as the reworked, revised, polished prose they might turn into. Further, when we are in the middle of working on our texts, we are constantly problem solving, so we are always looking for parts that need development or revision. We are in the business of finding faults to work on, so it is no wonder we become aware of many flaws, and may even despair of fixing them all. We are also aware of the devices we use to solve or sidestep these problems, and we may not feel fully confident in them, or we may feel that we are making only surface technical fixes and not addressing something deeper. In any event, because we are in the middle of the factory, watching the messy and contingent process by which texts are produced, we are aware of the difference between where our text is and where we would like it to be.

Finally, our awareness of the all these limitations of our emerging texts makes us aware of our own limitations as writers. We become aware that it would be good to be familiar with certain facts or theories we have not addressed or do not know in detail. We wish we had studied certain other models more deeply. We wish we were more skilled in finding creative organization, or finding fresher and more powerful metaphors or writing more focused and incisive sentences. This awareness of our own limitations can be compounded by beliefs about how others will judge us through our writing. By writing we put ourselves literally on the line, for others to evaluate our accomplishment. Thus as our text emerges toward final form, we can become even more unsure of how others might value our work and us. We may even fall into a kind of obsessive perfectionism, that if only we can make this text precise and perfect, it will overcome all of the uncertainties of audience and consequence to have exactly the effect we hope.

To move forward with our writing, however, we need to learn to live with our uncertainty and sense of limitation. There is no alternative, if we are to write and grow as writers, to keep on working despite our perception of our limitations. Every time we feel moved or need to write, we work from limited knowledge, limited skills, limited sense of the environment, with only guesses about the impact of our words on others and possible outcomes of events. While there are occasions when the situation of writing is so well known, shared and constrained that we can be fairly sure of the outcome, yet in many situations we must often act within deep uncertainty about the situation and anxiety about the outcome. Thus writing takes courage and a willingness to step forward despite risk and uncertainty.

We write with the skills and knowledge and resources we have now, and not the skills or knowledge we might have in five years. But we will not progress unless we keep working on the tasks in front of us. It is through confronting tasks, gathering the knowledge to pursue them, and solving the problems these tasks pose that we develop as writers, so that perhaps our work five years from now will be more advanced. We have to keep in the game. Yet making our peace with our limited skills and resources, does not relieve us from doing the best we can under the current circumstances—seeking the extra information if it is available, rewriting and reorganizing the draft if we see a better path, going over the drafts enough times from enough angles to be sure we have done the best we can do now—and then leaving it at that. You place your bets and take your chances.

BEING PREPARED FOR THE AFTERMATH

The text being finished does not mean the end of personal and psychological issues we have to deal with. First, particularly if the writing has required especially intense effort and problem solving, our relief at having finished may be mixed with less pleasant emotions. We may suffer a mental exhaustion, leaving us unable to concentrate on any mental work, especially other writing. We may even feel physically drained, even unable to engage in any kind of distraction. This may be further compounded if the writing has been the central focus of our thinking for an extended period, so we may not easily find something else to turn our attention to. This exhaustion and lack of distracting alternatives finally may lead to us to dwell on our anxieties about the text and what people may think about it. We may be filled with second thoughts and obsess about imagined faults.

Such feelings may lead us to hold on to the text long after useful work has been completed. Even after we send it to the editors, publish it to the blog, or hand it to our boss, we may be haunted with such thoughts. There is little to be done with such feelings except to recognize them as such and not get too upset by them or take them too seriously. Resting, turning attention elsewhere as emotional resources renew, and waiting for realistic responses before making any judgment about the text's effectiveness are all that can be done. After all, we have done the best we can do, and the rest is in the hands of others.

Often with writing we may get little or no response, which can be quite disappointing, increasing self-doubt about the value of our message or our skill in delivering it. This uncertainty may arise from something as simple as our not getting a response when we fill out an online form and getting no acknowledgment of our submission (Did we fill it out correctly? Will we get the product? Will our credit card be charged with inappropriate fees?) The uncertainty and disappointment becomes greater the more the writing reflects our extended work and thought. If no one, however, writes a response to an article, that does not mean in fact that no one has read it, thought about it, or was influenced by it. It is in the nature of writing that texts go out into the world often with little feedback or response returning to us.

On a smaller scale we feel such abandonment if we are participating on a list serve or a chatroom and the discussion goes on just as if we had never contributed. We seem not to have created a visible social fact that has changed the dialogic landscape. As writers we have to come to terms with this kind of inattention, and try to learn from it, to understand why our message seemed ineffective in order to make it more effective the next time, to wait for the right moment, to enter the discussion from a different angle, to make our message more pointed and forceful, or to enter with issues that might connect more to the other readers. We cannot let the rejection so discourage us that we do not attempt again, but rather understand that this is just a sign of how hard we have to work on effective writing to have an impact where we want it.

When others do respond, then we have further issues to deal with. We would like people to accept and understand our message just as we imagine it with all the emotion and importance we attribute to it, yet that often does not happen. The one place we are most likely to get response or feedback is in school, but the teacher's role is complicated. Often teachers feel the need to identify areas for correction, improvement, and instruction, or even evaluate our work for a grade. This may lead to many negative comments mixed in with the positive receptive comments. Teacher responses may make us fear all audiences will be constantly evaluating and correcting us. Even if teacher comments are positive and receptive, we know they are responding from a teacher's role rather than as someone who has practical, personal, or functional reasons to take our messages seriously.

If we submit something for publication, editors and reviewers, even if they like our manuscript and want to publish it, are likely to have suggestions for improving the text. While we sometimes may immediately appreciate the wisdom of these comments and begin to meet their concerns, we may well see the comments as misguided, foolish, or silly, perhaps even threatening the integrity and meaning of what we are trying to communicate. It is common for authors to respond with anger, sense of insult, and a strong to desire to give colorful labels to these editors and reviewers, no matter how tactfully the criticisms are phrased. Reporters have a saying: All editors are idiots; there are no exceptions. Yet editorial comments may sometimes actually be right on target and have touched a raw nerve or blindspot we have had. After some time to let the temper cool, it is worth rereading and thinking through exactly what is being suggested under the assumption that the reviewers are intelligent, well-intentioned people.

Even if the comments are in fact totally misguided and missing the text's meaning or ignorant of important contexts and background, we need to ask ourselves why those readers read your texts in such unexpected ways. Those editors and reviewers may well be indicative of our desired audience, and if they are misunderstanding or unjustly rejecting, we need to figure out why and how the text might be able to reach those readers, or at least counter the stated objections. The way readers understand and respond to a text is very important information and we should always be thankful for it, even if it at first we find it offensive. Part of developing a professional attitude toward writing is being able to see our writing in its larger communicative context and not assume that others ought to see things as we do. People's experiences, knowledge, beliefs and commitments are so various, that to reach them and activate their minds in ways that are receptive to our message may require much thought and skill, and any information we may get about how the message is received by different audiences, no matter how negative, helps us understand the challenges better.

When facing the text again for further revisions on the basis of feedback from teachers, editors, reviewers, or friends, it helps to look at the text through their eyes, to see what they have seen in it. This may mean significant changes in the text, rearranging orders of ideas, providing different entryways to bring readers in, offering them more guidance, or eliminating things that are obvious or irrelevant to them. It may even mean eliminating elements that we may be most attached to—because they represent idiosyncratic perspectives or phrasing that are more meaningful to us than to anyone else. If these meanings are essential to the text we may need to find a different way to express them and show their relevance and importance. At the very least, trying to take the position of the reader will give a deeper understanding of what the text does and does not accomplish for others, and how to make it more effective for them.

Then once our words are out there, we have to learn to live with what we have said, but yet see it as part of a long dialogue carried out over time. If we are fortunate enough to get specific response, it is likely not to be simply positive in adopting our views. People are more likely to respond if they have something to discuss or argue with or present an alternative to. So then we need to decide whether to respond immediately, not respond at all, or let the discussion evolve before we chime in again. And then if we respond, we need to find a constructive way to do so, even if we need to defend something we have previously written. We have to find a way to clarify and defend what we have put on the line without being defensive. But we should also be open to evolving our thoughts as a result of the dialogue.

Few texts are timeless. Some are read over more times than others. Some may be read actively for months or years, influencing ongoing discussions. Some live for a few moments then vanish maybe into archives, or maybe into the trash. Discussions and contexts evolve, modifying the meaning attributed to the text, providing opportunity to make further contributions, or taking ideas and work further. Those few works still read over centuries have different effect and different meanings in changing contexts and social concerns. Even sacred scriptures undergo changed interpretation in changing contexts and applications. We need to see our texts within the changing world they are part of and our own ability to say more. When we are writing, finishing the text seems to be an end in itself: we want it to say all we have to say on the subject, and to say it for all time. But if we are aware whatever we write as part of an evolving universe of meanings, we will have more equanimity as we write, and later as we see what happens to our text as it does or does not get filtered through other minds. We do not always have to be writing the final and permanent word. In fact, we never do.

REFERENCES

Austin, J. L. (1962). *How to do things with words.* Oxford: Oxford University Press.

Bakhtin, M. M. (1981) *The dialogic imagination.* Austin: University of Texas Press.

Bakhtin, M. (1984). *Problems of Doestoevsky's poetics.* University of Minnesota Press, Minneapolis.

Bakhtin, M. M. (1986). *Speech genres and other late essays.* Trans. by Vern W. McGee. Austin, TX: University of Texas Press.

Bazerman, C. (1994). Systems of genre and the enactment of social intentions. In A. Freedman, & P. Medway (Eds.), *Genre and the new rhetoric.* (pp. 79-101). London: Taylor & Francis.

Bazerman, C. (1999a). *The languages of Edison's light.* Cambridge, MA: MIT Press.

Bazerman, C. (1999b). Letters and the social grounding of differentiated genres. In D. Barton & N. Hall (Eds.), *Letter writing as a social practice* (pp. 15-30). Amsterdam: Benjamins.

Beale, Walter H. (1989). *A pragmatic theory of rhetoric.* Carbondale, IL: Southern Illinois University Press.

Becker, H. S., Geer, B., & Hughes, E. C. (1968). *Making the grade.* New York: John Wiley & Sons.

Bitzer, L. (1968). The rhetorical situation. *Philosophy and Rhetoric, 1,* 1-14.

Boice, R. (1990). *Professors as writers: A self-help guide to productive writing.* Stillwater, OK: New Forums Press.

Chafe, W. (1994). *Discourse, consciousness, and time: The flow and displacement of conscious experience in speaking and writing.* Chicago: University of Chicago Press.

Christensen, F. (1967). *Notes toward a new rhetoric.* New York: Harper & Row.

Connors, R. (1981). The rise and fall of the modes of discourse. *College Composition and Communication, 32,* 444-455.

Corbett, E. (1965). Classical rhetoric for the modern student. New York: Oxford University Press.

Crowley, S., & Hawhee, D. (1994). Ancient rhetorics for contemporary students. New York: Simon & Schuster.

Csikszentmihalyi, M. (1975). *Beyond boredom and anxiety: Experiencing flow in work and play.* San Francisco: Jossey-Bass.

Dias, P., Pare, A., Freedman, A., & Medway, P. (1999). *Worlds apart: Acting and writing in academic and workplace contexts.* Mahwah, NJ: Erlbaum.

Eastman, R. (1984). *Style: Writing and reading as the discovery of outlook* (3rd ed.). New York: Oxford University Press.

Fischer, C. (1992). *America calling.* Berkeley: University of California Press.

Fogarty, D. J. (1959). *Roots for a new rhetoric.* New York: Teachers College Press.

Goffman, E. (1981). *Forms of talk.* Philadelphia: University of Pennsylvania Press.

Goffman, E. (1974). *Frame analysis.* New York: Harper & Row.

Goody, J. (1986). *The logic of writing and the organization of society.* Cambridge: Cambridge University Press.

Halliday, M. A. K., & Matthiessen, C. M. (2004). *An introduction to functional grammar* (3d ed.). London: Arnold.

Hanks, W. (1996). *Language and communicative practices.* Boulder, CO: Westview.

Lanham, R. (1978). *Style: An anti-textbook.* New Haven: Yale University Press.

Marx, K. (1937). *The Eighteenth Brumaire of Louis Bonaparte.* Moscow: Progress Publishers.

Mead, G, H. (1934). *Mind, self, and society.* Chicago: University of Chicago Press.

Miller, C. R. (1992). Kairos in the rhetoric of science. In J. L. Kinneavy, S. P. Witte, N Nakadate, & R. Cherry (Eds.), *A rhetoric of doing* (pp. 310–327). Carbondale: Southern Illinois University Press.

Murphy, J. J. (1985). *Three medieval rhetorical arts.* Berkeley: University of California Press.

Parker, W. R. (1967). Where do English departments come from? *College English, 28,* 5, 339-351

Perelman, C. & Olbrechts-Tyteca L. (1969). *The new rhetoric: A treatise on argumentation.* Notre Dame: University of Notre Dame.

Puttenham, G. (1589). *The arte of English poesie.* London.

Sacks, H. (1995). *Lectures on Conversation* (2 vols.). Oxford: Blackwell

Schegloff, E. A., Jefferson, G., & Sacks, H. (1977). The preference for self-correction in the organization of repair in conversation. *Language 53,* 361-82

Schmandt-Besserat, D. (1992). *Before writing.* Austin: The University of Texas Press.

Searle, J. (1969). *Speech acts.* Cambridge: Cambridge University Press.

Stillar, G. (1998). *Analyzing everyday texts.* Thousand Oaks, CA: Sage.

Swales, J. (1990). *Genre analysis: English in academic and research settings.* Cambridge: Cambridge University Press.

Tannen D. (1993). *Framing in discourse.* NY: Oxford University Press.

Thomas, W. I. (1923). *The unadjusted girl.* Boston: Little, Brown & Co.

Tiersma, P. (2010). *Parchment, paper, pixels.* Chicago: University of Chicago Press.

Volosinov, V.N. (1973). *Marxism and the philosophy of language.* Cambridge, MA: Harvard University Press.

Vygotsky, Lev. (1986). *Thought and language* (Alex Kozulin, Trans.). Cambridge, MA: MIT Press.

Williams, J. & Colomb G. (2010). *Style: Lessons in clarity and grace* (10th Ed). New York: Longman.

Lightning Source UK Ltd.
Milton Keynes UK
UKHW012123170822
407448UK00003B/791

9 781602 354739